The Happy Lifestyle

The Happy Lifestyle

BY

DR. CHRISTINE RENEE

HAR PUBLISHING, LLC
USA

First Edition 2017, Printed in the United States of America

ISBN: 978-0-9986296-0-5
Library of Congress Cataloging
LCCN: 2017917747

This book is dedicated to my mother who has demonstrated all throughout her life how to be happy despite any and every situation. She was the first person who taught me the virtues of being happy no matter what life hands me. I would also like to dedicate this book to all those that shall read it; to the future generations; and to anybody that might be searching for happiness. This book is for you!

CONTENTS

PREFACE

This book came about because of a desire to help people understand that they can be happy regardless of their situation and or status in life. This book also came about because of a desire to help people fulfill their destiny. And to help people understand that their situation, people, places, and things do not dictate one's happiness.

The information in this book is from personal experience as well as from general observations on what it takes to live a happy life; and how to stay happy. Throughout these pages I go into practical details and applications on how one can obtain genuine happiness. You'll find this book essential and necessary for your everyday life and for the rest of your life. Hope you enjoy reading it as much as I have enjoyed writing it and living it. Now get ready to embark upon *The Happy Lifestyle*.

ACKNOWLEDGEMENTS

I would like to acknowledge Christ who has caused me to know peace, love, joy, and happiness despite all the many tests and trails that I have been through. It is because of my relationship with Him. I have been able to maintain being happy and not bitter throughout the years.

I would also like to acknowledge all my social media platforms, friends, and family. For everyone in my network that have been gracious enough to listen to, to like, to share, and respond to all my happy post and updates.

It is because of my social media platforms that I have been able to reflect and exam what happiness really is. If it were not for my social media platforms. I don't think this book would have ever come about.

I'm also grateful for and would like to acknowledge all my spiritual mentors, teachers, and associates that have helped mold and shape me into the *happy* woman that I am today. Too many to name, nevertheless, thank you.

Know yourself and make sure you know what it takes to make you happy. You'll be surprise at how it's just the little things in life that really matters.

Dr. Christine Renee

1

INTRODUCTION TO THE HAPPY LIFESTYLE

Nobody wants to be miserable, distraught, angry, sad, mad, frustrated, or discussed. Just about everyone wants to live a life free from adversity and drama. Living a life full of happiness on a consistent basis is one of the greatest achievements ever. And make no mistake about it, no man, woman, drugs, or amount of money can really make you happy.

The practical information and problem-solving skills throughout this book will help one stay focused in their pursuit of happiness. As you read each chapter, you'll discover what happiness is and why every human being desires it. You'll discover what it takes to make you happy. What distracts you from happiness and what causes you to become *unhappy*. You'll also learn how to avoid distractions. How to press forward in conquering problems. And how to maintain happiness despite any adversities, tests, and trails. The happy lifestyle is a remarkable lifestyle full of peace and joy. And it is obtainable!

The United States Declaration of Independence consist of the famous phrase, which I like to call the hook. Where it states, every human being has the right to life, liberty, and the pursuit of *happiness* as designed by God and protected by the government. This is a wonderful declaration. However, it appears many people in America and abroad are living a life full of adversity, full of problems, unresolved conflict, strife, wars, rumors of wars, cultural divisions, anger, and agony. I believe it's because many are looking to all the wrong people, systems, wrong places, and going through all the wrong motions to obtaining happiness.

Despite all the negativity in the world one must understand being happy on a consistent basis is a *choice*. It is a life long journey. Life doesn't guarantee anyone happiness nor does the Declaration above. One must pursue happiness at all cost and develop a state of mind that is conducive to making happiness achievable. As you read each chapter here are some of the key points to remember:

> Being happy is *not* just a matter of saying your happy. Happiness can be a reality.

> Happiness is a matter of choice, no matter what you may be going through. You choose to happy.

➤ Being open minded and thinking positive is key to happiness.

➤ Never ever give up on being happy.

➤ Being happy is the only way to living a fulfilling and successful life.

The mind is the psychology of who we are and how we think. The mind processes the way we react to situations, people, places and things. The mind frames our thought patterns and it is the platform from which we develop life habits. Our daily thoughts are a result of the things we learned from the past. Things we're learning now in the present. And things in the future. Daily impressions of people, places, and things influence every area of our lives. Whether good, bad, negative, or positive the mind governs who we are.

As a man thinketh in his heart so is he (Proverbs 23:7). And the good thing about this is. Once you become an adult you get to choose what you think and what's good for your well-being. In retrospect, you get to choose to be happy by the way you think.

You can master your thoughts. You have to begin to train your mind to think happy thoughts. And realize you can be happy despite who you know; who you don't know; what you have; what you don't have. You can be happy no matter what. But it starts with the heart and mind.

Exercise your mind to think positive. Think on things that are uplifting and focus on things that are good. This will help you to become grateful and to be content with everyday living. This will also help you to become aware and understand that your life isn't as bad as it seems. There is always someone worst off then yourself. So, never under estimate the power of your thoughts as it relates to living a fulfilling and happy life.

It's unfortunate that most people in society have become co-dependent and satisfied with a pseudo happy life. Co-dependent on someone else or something else to *"make"* them happy. This type of thinking and expectation is unrealistic. Thinking like this can also cause grief and possibly set ones-self up for a slow demise.

Your happiness is your responsibility and not anyone else's. Other people can contribute to and add to your happiness. But the ultimate goal and responsibility is yours. People, places, things, and institutions may let you down. But genuine happiness that comes from within will never let you down. Being positive and having a positive outlook on life all starts from within yourself.

Happy Note: Each day brings about different challenges. Which almost makes it impossible to be happy every moment... However, practicing happiness each and every day is the goal.

You have to set aside time every day and reflect on the good and positive things that are going on in your life. Start appreciating all the many blessings that come your way. Remember it's the little things in life that makes the difference. Learn how to be content in whatever state you are in. Because contentment is great gain.

I have discovered true happiness is obtainable. And I hope after you read this book, you'll have a better appreciation for what true happiness is. Set *goals* for yourself as you read each chapter. At first this may seem difficult, because you may have become accustomed to thinking negative. However, as you progress throughout each chapter. You'll began to notice a change in your thinking and in your lifestyle as it pertains to being happy.

While you're on this *journey* don't get discouraged. Use this book as a reference. Read it again and again if you have to. Use this book as a guide and practice being happy on a consistent basis. Because happiness is a pursuit! And as you begin to pursue happiness. Pursue it all cost. Learn to be happy in whatever state you are in. Court happiness as if your life depends on it! As so, it does.

Happy Key Points to Remember:

- ➤ Pursue happiness at all cost.

- ➤ Practice and master being happy.

- ➤ Train your mind to think happy thoughts.

- ➤ Genuine happiness is obtainable.

- ➤ Think positive and happy thoughts every day.

- ➤ Write down happy goals.

- ➤ Take responsibility for your own happiness.

Being happy is a mark of sheer joy and pleasure!

11

HAPPY DESPITE ADVERSITY

This chapter focuses on how to be happy in the mist of adversity, and how to live the happy lifestyle despite situations and or circumstances. Tests and trials are a part of life and nobody escapes them. Adversity happens to us all. Tests and trails show up unexpectedly and tries to rob us of any happiness that we may have. Test and trails also come to shorten our life expectancy, if we do not handle them properly. Being happy despite tests and trails is truly a gift that can be mastered.

Life can be very challenging especially when things go wrong and don't work out as expected. We can easily get into a self-pity mode and a victim's mentality. We can also become offended and defensive at people. Bitter and angry as well. Rather than pursue happiness in the moment. Many of us sitcom to a life rooted in past defeats and failures. Some will even try any and everything to try to take away the pains of yesterday. Yet, some make good and others live their lives to the best of their ability.

Learning to obtaining happiness in the mist of adversity is going to be one of the most difficult yet important things you do in life. When things are going well and when things are not going well. You'll have to remember it is your responsibility to choose to be happy. Remember trouble does not last forever and adversity can lead to opportunities. You know the old saying, when life hands you lemons... learn to make lemonade.

Happy Note: One must have an innate ability to face adverse circumstances and look at them as opportunities.

Whenever you're going through a difficult time. Get alone and confess with your mouth and believe in your heart that everything is going to be alright. Whatever you may be going through, remember this too shall pass. Learn to confess, that you are going to be happy no matter what you might be going through. Truly believe all things are working together for your good!

Happy Note: One of the secrets to living the happy lifestyle is to remember trouble comes, but eventually it goes away. Choose to be happy no matter what and have a grateful attitude and heart towards God. Knowing He is going to work everything out for your good.

There are several different things you need to know, in order to be happy and stay happy in the mist of adversity. First and foremost, you must be willing to make being happy a *priority* in your life. Ecclesiastes 3, King James Bible version says, there is a time and a season for *every* activity under the heavens:

A time to be born and a time to die;

A time to plant and a time to uproot;

A time to kill and a time to heal;

A time to tear down and a time to build;

A time to weep and a time to laugh;

A time to mourn and a time to dance;

A time to scatter stones and a time to gather them;

A time to embrace and a time to refrain from embracing; A time to search and a time to give up;

A time to keep and a time to throw away;

A time to tear and a time to mend;

A time to be silent and a time to speak;

A time to love and a time to hate;

A time for war and a time for peace.

These are words of wisdom. Because adversity can be very difficult to handle. Troubled times will make you think you are the only one going through what you are going through. Therefore, it is your responsibility to strive towards the goal of being happy no matter what. It is your responsibility to realize there is no greater goal than happiness.

Muster up all the positive energy you can for every season in your life. Know what season you are in and get understanding while you're in it. Whether the season is good or bad. There is a purpose for everything. There will be plenty of opportunities for you to learn from. And for you to make the necessary adjustments from any bad choices you may have made.

Regardless to what season you are in. Live a happy and fulfilling life. Because seasons come and they go. Therefore, deep down within your spirit and in your soul. You going to have to believe everything is going to be alright.

As stated before, it's not anyone else's responsibility or priority to make you happy. In order for you to be authentically and genuinely happy it must start from within and work its way out. You can be perfected. You can be happy and exhibit happy behaviors and characteristics. Seek out positive ways to maintain happiness no matter what. And no matter how people mistreat you. It is still your obligation to pursue happiness at all cost.

Someone might be saying, "how can I be happy when I lost a child in a bad accident; my mother died; I never knew my father; and my spouse left me"? Glad, you asked. All these things are horrible and I empathize with you. However, the good thing is, you don't have to come to ruins because bad things happen. You don't have to become bitter to the point you feel like you want to end your life. Have hope in God and allow Him the privilege of helping you in the mist of tribulations. Seek wise counsel and get counsel from someone you trust and can talk to.

Although your happiness is priority. No one is saying you shouldn't feel sad, sorry, or grieved about certain situations, circumstances, or mishaps. However, you mustn't drown yourself in sorrow. Let *not* your future happiness be forsaken or forgotten. Life happens! Bad things happen to us all. Let me let you in own a secret. Sometimes life is not fair! But God is able to restore onto you the joy of His salvation, if you let Him.

Test, trials, and situations may be your reality for now. This may be a difficult season you are in. But trust God in the mist of it all. Choose to be happy even if you don't understand what is going on or how you got into the predicament that you are in. Worrying never solves anything.

Even if your situation doesn't change as fast as you would like it to. You can still have hope knowing God is for you and *not* against you. He is waiting for you to come to Him. So, He can help you get you through whatever it is you're going through. The Bible says, after you have suffered a while God will establish you from any lost or grievances (1 Peter 5:10).

God is for you. He is on your side. He can heal your emotional state of being and your physical state of being as well. You being happy is not only beneficial for yourself. But for the benefit of those around you as well. Your children, your spouse, family members, coworkers, colleagues, associates, etc. are all connected to your happiness. Your happiness makes for a better environment. However, your happiness should *not* be predicated upon them *"making"* you happy, nor you *"making"* them happy. Even though we live in a society where most people long for affirmation. Happiness has to come within.

It is possible for others to contribute to your happiness without you being co-dependent on them or them being co-dependent on you. Affirmation from others is a good thing. We must *always* strive to get along with other people. But don't expect people to be God and don't you try to be God to them. You can only please people to a certain extent. As an adult you must never confuse being happy based on affirmation and confirmation from others. As an adult you should bring happiness to the table. And understand other people's affirmations are just an added bonus!

Happy Note: Everyone should be looking out for the best interest of others. However, we should never depend on others to make us happy.

Happiness shouldn't come at the expense of anyone else. If we can get this right. A whole lot of marriages, work relations, and race relations would be healthier, happier and easier to manage.

Happy Thought: *Being happy can bring you peace and a confidence that nobody can take away from you.*

If you are happy then other people in your life will be indirectly affected by your happiness.

Many have been dealing with sadness for a longtime. Some have gone through and are going through some very difficult situations, issues, struggles, and battles that never seem to end. Opposition, adversity, and persecution comes to rob you of peace.

Remember there is nothing you can do about the past. However, there is something you can do about the future. Seek professional counseling if needed. Confide in close family and friends if you must. But most importantly seek out godly counsel and wisdom from someone you can trust that will help you heal from past wounds and pain. You are the captain of your life, not your past. You are the only person that has the power to take control of your destiny; to the point that it produces a happy lifestyle for you now and in the future.

Happy Note: *The bible is full of scriptures and prayers to help you get through difficult situations. Google Christian counselors for counseling. Also, Google 24-*

hour prayer-line ministries that can pray with you and for you.

Dealing with issues on a daily basis can make you feel insecure and feel like a target for trouble. Left feeling like a victim of despair. Thinking nobody has gone through what you have gone through. All these things can be downright overwhelming. In most cases just getting along with other people can be very trying at times.

We all have our share of troubles. Every person at one time or another goes through curtain situations and difficult times. But don't let tough times define you. Someone once said, "trouble comes to make you", as in make you stronger. Sometimes tough times can be an opportunity and a blessing in disguise. Many entrepreneurs and inventors evolve during tough seasons. You never know what your made of until you go through something.

Therefore, make up in your mind that nothing is worth losing your happiness. Every adversity can be an opportunity for you. During tough times the opportunity is for you to learn something. Learn something about your character and the character of others as well.

It can also be a time for you to draw closer to God and the things of God. To re-evaluate your life and see if there's anything in your life you must let go of so, you can move to the next level.

During difficult times it is best to try to be happy in-spite of the situation.

My Testimony: I've been through some very difficult and trying times myself. However, you would never know it unless I told you. I have a testimony just like most people. And I have fought many battles just like most people have. Behind closed doors, I've cried many tears and felt so alone that it felt like I was going to lose my mind. I have also been so angry at God, to the point, I thought He had forsaken me. But through it all, I've kept the faith. With many years of practice and learning to repent, pray, and praise. I can now say, "I choose to be happy despite adversity". I have persevered and learned the lessons in most situations. And I know God has never left me nor forsaken me. He has always been there for me, waiting for me to trust Him.

Happy Note: As you learn to practice happiness, you'll begin to find that problems and situations are just stepping stones to a happier and better life.

The Bible says, the joy of the Lord is our strength (Nehemiah 8:10). Therefore, we can draw from God's joy even when we feel sad, mad, hurt, and depressed. God's joy comes to make us strong when we are weak. To give us inner peace through the guidance of Holy Spirit, who leads and guides us into all truth. The infilling of Holy Spirit is enough to make one happy. He is the Spirit of God as referred to the Comforter (John 14:26). He comes to comfort all that ails us and to give everlasting joy.

Happy Note: Make this your declaration: that you are going to be happy despite any and every situation. Speak out-loud and declare that you are not going to let anything, nor anyone hinder you from achieving happiness.

In all things one must be realistic in the pursuit of happiness. Because every day is not going to be a happy day, unless you choose to be happy. Bad things happen to good people and bad people alike. It's a part of life. Learning to be happy on purpose, is the goal. You must come to a point that you realize that nothing in life is guaranteed and all the other stuff in between living and dying must be dealt with.

Always use wisdom and be real when dealing with issues that you think are hindering you from being happy. Each one of us face problems and issues. But being happy is better than being sad. Happiness is a positive force that will help you overcome any and every obstacle. Practice looking at situations and adversity as a tool for learning to survive in life. Let nothing hinder you from your pursuit.

Happy Note: *Most everything we do in life is geared towards obtaining happiness. Our choice of careers, hobbies, spouses, relationships, and a host of other things. Happy is the goal! When dealing with issues we must remember the proverbial phrase, "when life situations hand you lemons... learn to make lemonade"! Meaning turn something bitter into sweet. Adversity into opportunity.*

Happy Key Points to Remember:

➤ Learn to be happy despite adversity. Because adversity, test and trails happen to us all.

➤ Practice finding peace and happy when things are going well and when things are not going well.

➤ Trouble comes, but eventually it goes away.

➤ When things are not going well that's the time to *choose* to be happy.

➤ Make being happy a priority and a duty in your life.

➤ Your happiness should never be predicated upon someone else making you happy.

Happy Reflections

*Happiness is when you're happy
and everyone around you
know your happy!*

III

FEELS GOOD TO BE HAPPY

You know the saying, "Happy Go Lucky"? Well, I have a similar saying that I think is much better and it goes like this . . . "It feels good to be happy". I have said this so many times that its actually helped heal me in areas where I was grieving. Even when I'm hurting deep down in my heart and do not feel happy. I say it anyways. Regardless to how I feel. Moral of the story is, you can't wait until everything in your life is perfect. You must think happy and say your happy no matter what you may be going through!

Thinking happy and saying your happy is one of the greatest assets you'll ever have in difficult situations. Happiness is a feeling of pleasure. It also means:

➢ Contentment
➢ Delighted
➢ Pleased
➢ Glad
➢ Excited
➢ Cheerful

- ➢ Cheery
- ➢ Merry
- ➢ Joyful
- ➢ Jolly
- ➢ Fortunate
- ➢ Favorable advantageous
- ➢ Opportune

Take a moment and think *realistically.* Is it possible to be happy *all* the time? If you have God in your heart, it can be. God has given each one of us an abundant supply of joy and happiness. So, if you make up your mind that you're going to walk in true spirituality, knowing with God all things are possible. It won't be hard to wake up every morning without joy.

Happiness is a way life! And when you really feel good and happy you exuberate positive energy and positive vibes. A feeling is anything that comes and goes and gives an emotional state or reaction to situations and or circumstances. However, sometimes life can leave us feeling overwhelmed and feeling like true happiness is un-obtainable. But even when you feel low, down, and distraught. God has given us the ability to draw from the rivers of joy imbedded within. The rivers of joy that flows from God's Spirit to ours.

One of the characteristics of God is joy. Therefore, make up in your mind that you're going to have joy and peace that only

God can give, through His Spirit (See Galatians 5:22). Having joy deep down in your heart is like being calm in a storm. Although the storms of life come. Let your testimony be, "I trust God" and "It feels good to be happy" in Him.

Many things are going on in the world today and many are facing difficult and challenging situations. So much so, *true* happiness has almost become a commodity. There are many things that comes to try you daily. Trouble comes to side track you and make you feel insecure about the future. People often ask me, "how can a person be truly happy when, so much pain and suffering is going on in the world"? And I respond by saying, "It takes individual effort, self-consciousness, and a choice to be happy". We'll talk more in depth about this in chapter six, *"I'm Happy Even When I Should Be Sad"*.

Feeling happy is a good thing. But it doesn't mean you're not concerned about what's going on in the world. It just means that your perspective on any given situation is different from the norm. I love people, but sometimes loving people can cause great pain. Especially from those that are closest to you. It's easy to put up a guard to try to protect yourself from getting hurt. But I've learned, in-order to be truly happy and feel happy. I must be willing to let down my guard, be vulnerable and fill my heart and mind with positivity on a consistent basis (See Romans 5:5 and 1 Corinthians 13).

You can't afford to walk around bitter and offended all the time. It's time to stop being so offensive because of past hurts. Expect God to heal you, so you can be happy. You might not feel happy about some things. However, focus on the positive things in life. Focus on things that give you a sense of satisfaction and things that make you happy.

As I write this chapter. I'm dealing with a couple of issues and situations in my own life. In this season of my life, I find I'm often misunderstood. I try to understand and to be understood. But sometimes it doesn't turn out that way. Being a Christian and a minister can be very lonely at times. However, I choose to not be distracted from being happy. I can't let what people feel or say about me affect me in anyway. I try not to let issues and situations affect my happiness. Because if I did, I would be one miserable person.

In the society we live in today. It's almost impossible to not be misunderstood. If you're going to take a stance for what you believe. You must be willing to be critiqued and criticized. Realizing people are not always going to be for you. But God has your back if your ding what He has called you to do. And if you're standing for what is good within moral reasoning. God will always help you and mature you into all things that pertain to your life. Regardless what others think or say.

In difficult situations I have learned to draw closer to God through prayer and meditation of scripture. I've learned to draw from within and tell myself, God loves me and I'm going to be happy. I also tell myself everything is going to be alright, regardless what the situation or circumstance may look like, this too shall pass. Every day is an opportunity to awake and be ready to face challenges and choosing to be happy because God is on your side.

Having the ability to practice being happy in every situation is truly a gift. Feelings of self-doubt, hatred, loneliness, lack, bitterness, grief, self-pity, etc., are all sufficient reasons to not feel happy. However, you must recognize that there will always be something or someone to make you feel unhappy. Therefore, your reaction to problems must be appropriated with choosing to not look at the things which are seen but choosing to look at the things which are unseen. Because the things which are seen are temporary and they are subject to change (2 Corinthians 4:18).

Even in your worst state you can truly have something to be happy about. Take heed to those words in 2 Corinthians 4:18 and put your feelings in check next time you feel sad, mad, depressed, and unhappy. Recognize when feelings of unhappiness come it's usually coming from the enemy of your soul. The negative voice within telling you that your situation is bad and your lot in life is downhill. That you have no other choice but to "feel" sad, mad, depressed, and unhappy. This is when you must take responsibility and be willing to take into consideration that things could be a lot worse. You're going to have to choose to be happy. There will always be something happening in your life. There will always be someone worst off then yourself. It's important for you to learn to *not* let situations or circumstances over take you.

There are spiritual forces in the atmosphere that are plotting your demise and trying to steal your happiness. For instance, there's a biblical scripture that says, for we wrestle not against flesh and blood (not against people). But we wrestle against spiritual wickedness (evil forces) in high places (Ephesians 6:12).

People are not always the problem nor are they responsible for how you feel. Because if you think about it. A person really doesn't have that much power or ability to *make* you feel happy. You will have to contend with seeking wisdom on how to deal with evil forces that may come up against you.

Proverbs 3:13-18 says:

Happy is the man that finds wisdom and the man that
gets understanding. For the merchandise of it is better
than the merchandise of silver and the gain thereof
than fine gold. She is more precious than rubies: and
all the things thou canst desire are not to be compared
unto her. Length of days is in her right hand; and in her

left-hand riches and honor. Her ways are ways of
pleasantness, and all her paths are peace. She is a tree
of life to them that lay hold upon her and happy is
every one that retains her.

Wisdom defines who we are and wisdom defines how happy we
can be. Wisdom will look sadness in the face and say I have so
much to be thankful for, and I choose to be happy.

It feels good to be happy is not based on actual feelings per
say. Because, feelings are fickle and feelings are fleeting. Feelings
come and feelings go. The human intellect and emotional state of
being is always changing. Therefore, you must look within, and let
the Spirit of God help you with your feelings. You must also watch
how you react to people, situations, and things that may be
provoking or triggering you. Your reaction to everything in life
must be guarded. Because your reaction effects how you deal with
negative situations.

Feelings were given to us by God. But it is your
responsibility to channel your feelings in a positive way. If you're
the type of person that is easily offended. You probably will have
to work at staying positive and not letting people get to you. Don't
let anyone rub you the wrong way and cause you to get side-
tracked and offended. Because being easily offended is a type of
pattern that will lead to you feeling negative and unhappy. From

now on practice overcoming the challenge of taking the bait of offense.

Feeling good and happy is not an automatic thing for most people. Let's face it, we live in a negative society. Just turn on the daily news media. After you have finished watching it, you may feel sad and disgruntled. Only because most news outlets report bad news more so than good new. Which can leave you feeling hopeless. Therefore, you must *practice* discarding negative feelings by projecting your feelings to something positive. As I stated earlier in this chapter. Even when you don't feel happy. You must make-up your mind that you are going to be happy no matter what. Then and only then will you discover true happiness.

You must realize happiness is a life's journey. It feels good to get up every day and take that journey and make that choice. Choosing to be happy means your happiness isn't based upon what is going on in the moment. But it stems from having a heart of gratitude for all the things you do have to be grateful for and happy about.

If you choose to be sad, down, defuncted, and depressed then you might as well get ready to be sad, down, defuncted, and depressed. Now don't get me wrong you will have days that you will not feel like even getting out of the bed. Some of you may feel that way right now. Sometimes this it's okay because your human. Having those feelings could be a sign that your body needs rest.

And rest is a good thing. But staying in bed all the time and depressed all the time is not good at all. If you feel this way all the time then you may need to seek professional counseling or medical advice. This may be the route you may need to go if you are constantly depressed all the time.

However, choosing to be happy, is what's going to *help* you feel better. If you have been diagnosed with clinical depression or have bouts of depression. By all means please continue seeking medical attention. But try incorporating a little laughter in your daily regimen. Because laughter is good for you. And the Bible says, laughter is good medicine (Proverbs 17:22).

Look at yourself in the mirror and tell yourself daily.... "I'm prosperous, healthy, and happy in every area of my life". And watch how much better you feel. Go a step further and get up every day and put your best foot forward to being happy. Get dressed, comb your hair, fix yourself up, and tell yourself... "*self I am happy and it sure feels good to be happy*"!

Also stay away from negative people that are always negative, sad, mad, or discussed about life or anything in general. Hanging around these types of people will defeat your chances of feeling positive and happy. Hang around people that are happy, positive, and have a successful outlook on life! You have the power to choose who you allow in your space.

Feeling happy is not the same thing as being immune to what's really going on in the world. But when you feel happy it brings about a sense of peace in your life. Always be concerned about your surroundings. But also, have a sense in knowing that situations don't have to have control over you and your thought pattern daily. You must learn to control your feelings. The Bible says we are to cast down every imagination and everything that exalts its self against the knowledge of God (2 Corinthians 10:4-6). And believe me God wants you happy. He is *not* in the business of making you *feel* sad and depressed. You have the power to feel happy.

Happy Note: From this day forward confess, "it feels good to happy"! And say it even if you don't feel like it. This is a sure sign; you are on your way to truly living a happy lifestyle.

Happy Key Points to Remember:

- You can't wait until everything in your life is perfect to feel happy.

- Happiness is not *just* a feeling; happiness is a choice and a way of life.

- You must choose to feel happy despite any situation and or circumstance.

- Feelings were given to you by God. But how you channel your feelings is your responsibility.

- Stay away from negative people and hang around people that are positive and happy.

- When you feel happy it brings about a sense of peace in your life.

- You have control over your thought pattern and your feelings.

Happy Reflections

_____

_____

_____

_____

_____

_____

_____

_____

Smile! It signifies you're happy.

Learn to be happy with whom God created you to be.
Love God and He'll help you succeed at being
a-more-better and happier you.

IV

HAPPINESS COMPARED TO BEING RICH & FAMOUS

We all need the basic-necessities like food, water, clothing, and shelter to live. However, people that are genuinely happy do not necessarily need extravagant possessions or things to make them happy. Having material possessions and/or wealth is nice. However, before you seek to be rich and famous. Please make sure you are happy within yourself first. Because people seem to have a misconception, that people that are rich and famous are always happy because they have money. I beg to differ.

One should not equate having money or things, to having genuine happiness. Money is not always a determining factor to happiness. Nor is money a compass to happiness. Money lays a significant part. However, money is just an ends-to-a-means.

Your happiness shouldn't be predicated upon how much money you have or don't have. Nor should your happiness be predicated upon how famous you are. Always strive to be the best that you can be. However, your happiness should be a direct correlation of your stability in life. And your ability to be happy regardless what your status in life is.

Don't get me wrong! I am not advocating poverty nor am I saying, one needs to poor to be happy. However, many people are looking to the rich and famous and saying, "wow if only I had all that money and fame, I would be happy". I say to you, "not necessarily". Being rich and famous can make you happy as well as unhappy if you let it. Money is just a tool in which we survive and thrive economically. And if you think being rich and famous is going to *make* you happy then you might what to reconsider what being happy really is.

If you happen to be rich and famous and you're reading this chapter. Please don't disregard what I am about to say. This chapter may or may not be for you. However, if it is for you. You will be able to bear witness to the points that I'm about to make.

True happiness is a state of mind. And if you tell yourself that on a consistent basis then you'll be happy. Because in reality you can be poor and miserable; and or rich and famous and miserable. The choice is yours. As we discussed earlier and as I keep reiterating. You must choose to be happy regardless of your status is in life. Again, I'm not advocating poverty. And I am not against wealth and prosperity. I am advocating that you should be working towards living happy and prosperous in life regardless to your affiliations and or economic status. Because true prosperity means being confident, secure, comfortable, whole, happy, etc...

Having money is a blessing. And even the Bible says, money answers all things (Ecclesiastes 10:19). But you mustn't get so caught up in having wealth, riches, and fame, that you forget true happiness comes from within. Money can't buy genuine happiness. Because there are some people with money, wealth, riches, and fame, but they are unhappy inside. Therefore, don't ever think authentic and genuine happiness is about having position, possession, and things.

Most of the time having money, fame, and or fortune just means having more responsibility. And this can often lead to having more problems in life. People that have obtained a sense of wealth and power respectively have their own share of stresses, pains, and strains that they have to deal with. This can lead to an everlasting effect of *unhappiness*. So, whether you're poor, rich, known or unknown you can still be happy.

We all know people who have worked very hard to obtain fame and fortune. And some have become mega superstars. And yet these same people have all kinds of issues that they must deal with. Some are just as miserable as the next person. And many have died an early age from all sorts of ailments and situations. And to me this is sad. Because even with all the money and mega iconic status. They still couldn't buy happiness.

Let's look at Hollywood and some of the people that represent the rich and famous. Just take a moment and look at how some are living. Many are living the so called rich and famous lifestyle. But facing some of the same problems and or issues that those who are not rich and famous are facing. Same problems. They get sick. They have marital and domestic problems if not more. Their children deal with issues and mishaps just like everybody else's children. And we know this to be true. But somehow, we still have this misconception that the rich and famous are happy or should be happy because they have money.

Those that are rich in business, famous in politics, and in the arts, all know fame and fortune comes with a price. Material things can never bring genuine happiness. Money shouldn't be the determining factor or sole source of your happiness. Your happiness must come from within you.

For what does it profit a man or woman to gain the whole world but lose his or her soul? God is not against riches and wealth. Matter of fact God gets happy when His people are blessed and prospering. But you can't sell your soul for wealth. Nor should your pursuit of happiness be rooted in money. You should have confidence knowing it is Gods will for you to be blessed and prosperous. And for you to walk in your divine purpose for your life.

God can bless you so good and give you an abundance of wealth with no sorrow (Proverbs 10:22). No sorrow as in suffering to get wealth. And no misery trying to obtain wealth. The joy of the Lord will overtake you when you're in the perfect will of God for your life and cause you to have peace and joy. There will always be good days and bad days. However. God has your back! Nothing the devil nor any other human being; or wicked force can do to stop Gods blessings for you.

Wouldn't it be wonderful if you didn't have to worry about money or position? Being able to focus on your purpose and being free to be all God has created you to be. Therefore, every person's goal in life should be to discover their purpose in life. And once you discover your purpose in life. Then fame and fortune will follow. Which results in true happiness. Every person's goal in life should be to discover their purpose and live it to the fullest. So, they can be happy.

Happy Note: Having enough money to meet your needs and wants and the needs of others is a wonderful thing. However, if this isn't your status right now, you can still be happy. Find out what it is that you've been called to do. Find your purpose in life and the money will follow. Discovering your purpose will also help you live a happy and fulfilling lifestyle.

Many people choose careers and mates that they do not like nor enjoy, all for money. It's a big mistake to take on a career that you are not equipped for or a mate that you do not love, all for the love of money. You will be miserable and everyone around you will be miserable as well. Never choose a career for money. I'll say it again, and again. Never ever choose a career for money.

The most miserable people on the earth are those that are working a job or in a profession that they do not have the passion and/or desire for. Especially if they are working or doing something for money and not for the sheer calling, enjoyment, and pleasure for.

It is imperative that you find your purpose in life. This may take time weeding out the wrong career choices. However, those that find their purpose and destiny in life tend to be a lot happier than those that do not know what they have been called to do. Know who you are; know what you represent; and know what you have to offer in life. And don't ever get caught up in comparing yourself to other people.

The bible says, God rains on the just and the unjust (Matthew 5:45). Meaning the grace of God is given to all to prosper. So be very careful and don't get caught up in judging others or being envious of what someone else has. Because the same God that caused them to obtain wealth and riches is the same God that will give you power to obtain wealth (Deuteronomy 8:18).

Happy Note: Never compare yourself nor your life to anyone else. Because you never know what a person has had to go through to get what they have accomplished. The bottom-line is... true happiness is knowing who you are and fulfilling your destiny and purpose.

Discovering your purpose has a lot to do with your ability to succeed and be happy. While some think having a job and a pay check with six figures is the ultimate goal to happiness. But if you are not confident and unhappy with your work. It will be very hard for you to enjoy a *pay check*. You'll spend most of your days miserable and dreading to go to work or a career that you hate.

Your next level and promotion in life shouldn't be predicated upon just having a paycheck. After you find out what it is that you like to do and what your purpose is, do it! Happiness can stem from being confident in doing what you do best. Confidence can be defined as:

➤ Trustworthiness in a person or thing.

➤ The feeling or belief that one can rely on someone or something.

➤ A firm trust, belief, faith, credence or conviction.

➤ A feeling of self-assurance, assertiveness, poise.

➤ Courage, boldness and nerve.

In society, there are many people doing great things and making great things happen. We tend to call these success stories or successful people. However, what I have noticed is most people we tend to regard as successful are hardworking and confident people. They know what they want, what they are called to do in life and they go after it. Having confidence, is a wonderful asset that can lead to fame, and fortune. But, if you don't have confidence in yourself, then how do you expect anyone else to have confidence in you?

Confident people may not be famous or rich. Yet their success speaks for them. They don't need to brag about their success. And most importantly confident people do not believe in failure nor do they have a *victim's* mentality. In other words, a confident happy person doesn't look to other people to make them feel successful or happy. Nor do they blame others for their failures. Whatever negatives life throws at them. They look at it as stepping stones or as an opportunity to do better.

Happy Note: Being happy and confident and doing what you've been called to do means staying away from negative people who try to make you feel less then what God has created you to be!

Happy is the man (woman, boy, girl) who put their trust in God (Psalms 40:4).

Happy Key Points to Remember:

➢ Your happiness shouldn't be predicated upon how much money you have or don't have.

➢ Money is just a tool in which we use to survive and thrive economically.

➢ You must choose to be happy regardless of what your monetary status is in life.

➢ Poverty has its own stresses, pains, and strains that can leave an everlasting effect of *unhappiness*.

➢ Authentic happiness comes from having peace of mind.

➢ It's a big mistake to take on a career that you hate or a mate that you don't love for money.

➢ Discovering your purpose has a lot to do with your ability to succeed and to be happy.

Happy Reflections

_____

_____

_____

_____

_____

_____

_____

As a man thinketh so is he.

Proverbs 23:7

V

HAPPY THOUGHTS

Happiness is a state of mind and being happy starts with the mind. Therefore, you must tell yourself you're going to be happy no matter what happens. Because as a man thinketh so is he. Get up every morning decreeing and declaring, you're going to be happy, and think happy positive thoughts. Because your mind will tell you to think of all the negative things that can and could go wrong, before you even start your day. Therefore, you must learn to think positive before you even get out of bed.

Think positive thoughts and say positive affirmations daily. Especially when you awake first thing in the morning. That's the time of day your thought pattern is fresh and not easily distracted. Do what you have to do and don't let the problems of the day, easily bombarded your mind. Do away with bad, negative thinking.

You must start each day thinking and believing good things are going to happen. Don't think about all the bad things that are going on in your life or in the world. Because most of the time your mind wants you to think the worst. Train yourself to think happy positive thoughts.

Medical science has proven some sicknesses and diseases are caused by certain foods we eat or by the why we think. Therefore, recognize some ailments are a direct correlation to the way you think. Your thought pattern is who you are. When you are facing difficult situations in your life, you must learn to trust God and choose to be happy no matter what. This is necessary and not based on feelings or emotions. Training your thought pattern. And learn to cast all your cares upon *Jesus*.

Happy Note: Learning to be happy and to remain happy is a beautiful thing. See Appendix II, it outlines declarations that you can speak out loud daily to decree your happiness.

Happiness brings strength and happiness will also help you cope with life's difficult situations. Therefore, as you move forward throughout your day think happy thoughts and remember:

➤ Happiness is the key to your success.

➤ Happiness is good for your health and laughter is good like medicine (a healing balm).

If you are going to be happy and live a happy lifestyle you can't afford to waste your thoughts. Don't be moved by your emotions or by what you see. In some instances, you can't be moved by what you hear either. Being happy is like walking by faith. Because walking by faith means not by sight (2 Corinthians 5:7).

Enemies, the devil, and evil forces are always roaming about seeking ways to devour. The bible says, the devil is the enemy; he is the accuser of the brethren; and the father of lies. Therefore, resist the devil and he will flee from you. Learn to cast *down* all imaginations and every thought that exalts its self against the knowledge of God. So, you can have peace and happiness.

There have been many days that I thought I was not going to make it. Where my mind would tell me to give up on God and myself. Negative thoughts bombarded my mind to try to make me feel depressed. But I *never* gave up on the promises of God. Every day you have to choose to not listen to the negative lies of the devil.

You must learn to get in the scriptures daily and choose to believe what Gods word has to say about you. And apply the word of God to every situation in your life. Philippians 4:8 says we ought to think on things that are true, noble, right, pure, lovely, admirable, excellent, and praiseworthy. These are just some of the things we should be thinking daily.

Likewise, we should always be conscious of current events and be mindful of national and worldwide events. However, let's face it the news media can be full of negativity and negative stereotypes. Most news media outlets are full of bias journalism and reporting. Their personal opinions and views of people, places, and things, can be right or wrong. In most cases, it seems like the news media is always trying to perpetuate hate, crime, violence, gossip, misfortunes and a host of other negative things that are going on in the world. It has been said that "bad" news sells. Therefore, most news media outlets seldom report *good* news. Sure, some reports are good. However, most people prefer to hear the negative gossipy updates, versus hearing the positive happy news.

You can't afford to let the news media dictate how your world view should be. Your joy and peace of mind is want's most important in this day and age. We must think on things which are above and not get infected by what the media and the world is doing or saying.

If you want happy thoughts to run through your mind on a consistent basis. Then you must monitor what you allow to filtrate through your mind daily. Be conscious of what types of information you process.

Whether the information is positive or negative, be cautious and filter out the negativity. This will help you have a more disciplined thought pattern. And will also help you filter out any hindrances that might be keeping you from obtaining a happy mind-set.

There is a lot of hatred and slander being published and spoken through bloggers, social media sites, and other media outlets like never before. Everyone seems to have an opinion of what they think should or should not be in certain situations or issues. However, your happiness shouldn't be based on the opinions of others.

The brain is a highly sensitive organ. God has created it to be affected by what it hears and by what it sees Therefore, be very careful what you entertain. If you're always listening to negativity. You'll be more prone to thinking negative thoughts. In general, whatever you reflect upon will become your perception or reality. Therefore, you must choose to reflect upon happy positive things.

The types of music you listen to can have a positive or negative impact upon you as well. Music can put you in a happy mood or a sad negative mood depending upon the lyrics. Music can influence your psyche for decades. So be careful what you allow through your ear gate. Listen to healthy music. Music with lyrics that are edifying and not toxic or degrading to your soul.

The human mind and intellect learn and memorizes through repetition. Through song and music more so than any other avenue. For instance, many of you can remember when you first learned the alphabet. You learned them through song and or by singing the *ABCs* repeatedly. The reason being is, the mind is more prone to grab hold of what it hears on a repetitive basis. What your mind hears can remains in your memory forever, especially when it's taken in through music and or singing.

Over the years there have been many things that I have purposely forgotten. However, when it comes to certain songs, I just can't seem to forget them. I was born in the sixties and I can *still* remember a lot of the old Motown songs. Some of the songs I haven't heard in years. However, after all these years if you ask me if I remember a certain song. More than likely, I'll say, "yes" and sing some of the lyrics.

This is the same for what we read and what we watch on television. I have this saying, *"garbage in... garbage out"*. Meaning whatever you indulge in negatively, through your eye and or ear gates, will have an impact on you subconsciously. Your thought pattern, reflects who you are. Therefore, you cannot take in negative *stuff* per say and expect to be happy.

Supposedly, we learn early in life what is right and what is wrong. However, society has produced a lot of negative programing that can have a tremendous impact on one's psyche and wellbeing. Children are exposed to way too much early in life. Things they should not be exposed to. As a child I was exposed to my share of negative things as well. Such as cursing (cussing, profanity), horror flicks, sexuality in *R*-rated films, etc... However, as an adult I have, had to learn to choose what is right and what is wrong for my wellbeing.

To be truly happy and positive one must also learn to let go of negative images from the past. This may be painful because you may still have memories of things that have left scars on your mind. However, you have to learn to trust God to help you forgive and to "forget" negative things from the past. Let go of mishaps and misfortunes. And if you must, seek counseling. There are good Christian counselors and professional counselors that have been trained to help you get delivered from negative painful memories of the past.

Leave the past behind and always forsake what is negative and detrimental to your happiness. Also remember whatever the enemy of your soul meant for your destruction, God can and will make it work together for your good. So, you can be free and help others heal and be happy. We all have a testimony of what we've been through and how we made it despite difficulties.

Just think about some of the things that you've made it through. Some of it should have killed you. Therefore, make every effort not to ever rehearse it again. Your testimony is your testimony. However, your authentic testimony should be, I made it and I'm *happy*!

Here are some practical things you can do to help you forget the past negatives; and help you live a happier life:

➤ Keep a journal and write down your own personal happy experiences and confessions.

➢ Declutter your surroundings and organize your home and work space. A more open clean environment with lots of fresh air and sunshine is refreshing, healthy and therapeutic.

➢ Volunteer and learn to give back to others. Because as you help others, you'll gain a sense of joy in knowing that you can be a blessing to someone else other than yourself.

➢ Try taking walks in the park or in areas where there's lots of scenery like flowers, trees, green grass, water, etc.

➢ Practice being in a quiet and peaceful setting with no sound for one to two hours a day. Turn off the television and radio and try reading a novel, biography, or just sit quietly.

➢ Attend church on a regular basis. Fellowshipping with other believers, is essential for your spiritual maturation and happiness.

➢ Exercise because physical exercise is good for your body, heart, soul, and mind. Physicians say, bodily exercise helps relieve stress.

➢ Listen to soothing music like classical, hymns, jazz, gospel, and worship. Because music affects your mood and whatever you listen to is what you'll become.

➢ Turn off the computer and the cell phone and spend time with family and friends.

➢ Spend time in prayer daily so you can be focused and revived.

➢ Relax your mind from all the things you can't do anything about.

➢ Read the Bible. Especially scriptures that relate to peace and joy. Appendix II has a list of scriptures that you can meditate upon.

➢ Get a manicure, pedicure, or a massage.

➢ Get a hobby and do things that you really enjoy doing. For example, fishing, golfing, tennis, baseball, basketball, reading, sewing, knitting, playing the piano or your favorite instrument, sailing, boating, skating, reading, shopping, traveling, camping, etc.

➢ Practice saving money. Saving money will help elevate some financial pressures and get you prepared for your future emergencies, future endeavors, and goals.

➢ Take a happy vacation at least once a year.

➢ Get proper rest and at least 6 hours of sleep at night. Also, learn to take naps occasionally, after a hard day's work.

➢ Practice making a list of things to do and writing things down so you can remember. Being organized is just half the battle to a fulfilling and happy lifestyle.

➢ Learn to walk in love and love your neighbor as yourself and try to pursue peace with all mankind (Hebrews 12:14). Your neighbor can be a family member, a neighbor next door, down the street, a co-worker, etc. This will help you to live a strife free and happy lifestyle.

➢ Don't let other people's drama or problems take you out of a stans of happiness. Learn when to say no and when to reach out to help others.

Every day is another day to get things right. Therefore, you don't have to walk around condemning yourself or having low self-esteem just because you've made a mistake. Or because of what has happened to you in the past. You must believe that there is no condemnation to those who are in Christ Jesus.

Happy Note: No one is perfect. Therefore, you do not have to live in condemnation. Some things you may or may not have had control over. But now is the time to let it go.

As I reflect upon my own life. I have done some foolish, crazy, outlandish things. Mostly because of lack of knowledge or lack of understanding. Or because I was immature in certain areas.

But if I had stayed stuck on the negative and continued to dwell on the past, I could have easily dwelled in condemnation.

Sometimes we say and do things that we regret. But thanks, be to God who gives us grace and mercy, so we can grow and mature in all things. God wants you happy. And He wants you to think good thoughts. It's never too late to get things right in your life. I don't care if your 80 years old or older! God can and will give you victory over the past so you can live a happy productive life.

Condemnation is a strong expression of disapproval of an action. It's also the act of declaring something awful, evil, or unspeakably, and to strongly disapprove of. By condemning someone or yourself it's like torment or punishment. Therefore, you need to put an end to condemning yourself and others. God has forgiven you and you must learn to forgive yourself. The Bible says in Roman 8:1:

There is therefore now no condemnation for those who are in Christ Jesus. For the law of the Spirit of life in Christ Jesus has set you free from the law of sin and of death. For what the Law could not do, weak as it was through the flesh, God sending His Son in the likeness of sinful flesh and as an offering for sin, He condemned sin in the flesh, so that the requirement of the Law might be fulfilled in us, who do not walk after the flesh but according to the Spirit.

No condemnation, means to be found innocent, not guilty of an accusation. Having no sentence inflicted and no guilty verdict found. Through God's grace He offers forgiveness. Now forgive yourself from every mistake and mishap from the past and move forward into the future.

Happy Note: Learn to be happy. Because we're all a work in progress and growing into becoming a better and happier person.

Happy Key Points to Remember:

➤ Being happy and staying happy starts with the mind.

➤ Think happy thoughts daily.

➤ Think on things that are true, noble, right, pure, lovely, admirable, excellent and praiseworthy.

➤ Get up every morning declaring and decreeing you are happy.

➤ For one to be truly happy and positive one must learn to get rid of and forsake all negative images from the past.

➤ Think on the positive things or the good things in life.

➤ Don't walk around condemning yourself or having low self-esteem just because you made a mistake.

➤ Forgive yourself and others.

Learn to be happy with who

God created you to be!

VI

I'M HAPPY WHEN I SHOULD BE SAD

Sadness is when you feel or show sorrow. Being sad and unhappy is a feeling that is subdued with feelings of sorrowfulness, dejected, depressed, oppression, downcast, miserable, despondent, despairing, disconsolate, desolate, wretched, glum, gloomy, doleful, dismal, melancholy, mournful, woebegone, forlorn, crestfallen, heartbroken, inconsolable and more. These types of things you must learn to shake off, so to speak. Sadness comes to us all at one point or another. To be happy when your sad sounds like an oxymoron. An oxymoron is a figure of speech which contradicts the way the terms is used in conjunction with. However, happy people can be the most joyful people to be around even when their hearts are heavy or sad.

With all that's going on in the world. There's a lot of things that'll make you feel sad. People can be cruel, harsh, and judgmental. And if you don't agree or conform to their point of view. They'll talk about you and be quick to put you down. It's sad. But as an individual you must be strong and stand firm in who you are and what you believe.

God has given us the truth through his word, the bible. Therefore, we can stand strong and have joy even in the mist of persecution. And when things are not going well. Stand for what is right and you'll eventually be happy for not conforming to what you know is wrong!

Happy Thought: Laugh out loud and laugh often. This helps keep your mind in a state of happiness. The goal is for you to think happy positive thoughts and speak out loud daily the affirmation at the end of this book. And most importantly never let what people say or think about you affect you negatively!

Have you ever met someone you knew was going through something difficult or grievous; but they still had a smile on their face? This is because happiness is a condition of the heart. Happiness is when you can laugh at your problems. Happiness is when your situation looks horrific, but you find peace and something to be glad about even in the mist of the storm. If the truth be told.

Happy people are not easily worried. Because they know worrying and being sad doesn't change things. Being sad only makes a negative situation or circumstance worst. Therefore, you must learn to ward off sadness and things that you have no control over. I'm not suggesting that you be unconcerned or callous. But you must be willing to fight off and cast down every thought that comes to steal and to kill your happiness. Learn to cast away everything that is contrary to you being happy within.

You must choose to be happy even when you're feeling sad. The bible clearly says, "the joy of the Lord is your strength". Sometimes things in life warrant sadness. For instance, the death of a loved one, calamities, financial mishaps, and so on. All these things can take a toll on you at some time or another. But happiness is still the goal and can be obtained even when you're not feeling up to "par".

Let's keep in mind that there are some medical conditions that warrant feelings of sadness. For instance, if you have chronic symptoms of sadness. Meaning you are sad for weeks, months or years. Then you may want to visit a physician for medical treatment for depression. However, do not negate seeking professional and biblical counseling as well. There are professional counselors available to counsel those that have grievances and for those who need spiritual healing (counseling). Make sure you get the proper help. Help that is suitable and based on deliverance from a medical and biblical perspective.

Remember you can look at any adverse situation and make the decision that you are *not* going to be a victim. But you're going to allow all things work together for your good. You might be saying how can anything good come out of what I am going through? Well I'm here to tell you, life is a series of advents; not all good and not all bad. However, it is important for you get all the lessons to be learned in the test and trails of life. And learn to take the good with the bad.

You must come to grips that "stuff" happens. But remember, just because "stuff" happens doesn't mean it's the end of the world. God is still in control and able to deliver you from any and every situation. He is always available in time of need. And He is waiting for you to cast all your cares upon Him because He cares for you (See 1 Peter 5:7).

Take a negative situation and turn it into a positive. This is definitely the way to live and the way to be happy! Here are somethings to meditate upon when you feel sad:

➤ Whatever is true, whatever is noble, whatever is right, whatever is pure, whatever is lovely, whatever is admirable—if anything is excellent or praiseworthy—think about such things (Philippians 4:8).

➤ The Lord himself goes before you and will be with you; he will never leave you nor forsake you. Do not be afraid; do not be discouraged (Deuteronomy 31:8).

- The righteous cry out, and the Lord hears them; he delivers them from all their troubles (Psalms 34:17).

- I waited patiently for the Lord; he turned to me and heard my cry. He lifted me out of the slimy pit, out of the mud and mire; he set my feet on a rock and gave me a firm place to stand. He put a new song in my mouth, a hymn of praise to our God. Many will see and fear the Lord and put their trust in him (Psalms 40:1-3).

- But you, Lord, are a shield around me, my glory, the One who lifts my head high (Psalms 3:3).

- Many are the woes of the wicked, but the Lord's unfailing love surrounds the one who trusts in him (Psalms 32:10).

- Why, my soul, are you downcast? Why so disturbed within me? Put your hope in God, for I will yet praise him, my Savior and my God (Psalms 42:11).

- I have told you these things, so that in me you may have peace. In this world, you will have trouble. But take heart! I have overcome the world (John 16:33).

- For I am convinced that neither death nor life, neither angels nor demons, neither the present nor the future, nor any powers, neither height nor depth, nor anything else in all creation, will be able to separate us from the love of God that is in Christ Jesus our Lord (Romans 8:38-39).

➤ Praise be to the God and Father of our Lord Jesus Christ, the Father of compassion and the God of all comfort, who comforts us in all our troubles, so that we can comfort those in any trouble with the comfort we ourselves receive from God (2 Corinthians 1:3-4).

➤ Dear friends, do not be surprised at the fiery ordeal that has come on you to test you, as though something strange were happening to you. But rejoice in as much as you participate in the sufferings of Christ, so that you may be overjoyed when his glory is revealed (1 Peter 4:12-13).

➤ The Lord makes firm the steps of the one who delights in him; though he may stumble, he will not fall, for the Lord upholds him with his hand (Psalms 37:23-24).

➤ So, do not fear, for I am with you; do not be dismayed, for I am your God. I will strengthen you and help you; I will uphold you with my righteous right hand (Isaiah 41:10).

Happiness is usually based upon what's happenings in your life. Whether things are going well or not. But joy is different from happiness. Joy is eternal, whereas happiness is a way of life. Joy is the revelation of eternal happiness, eternal delight, and eternal fulfillment that can only come from God. Even when you are sad. God will you give you joy in any and every situation if you trust Him. Draw from His joy today, because it is your strength (Nehemiah 8:10).

Joy is like a river that is deep down in your soul. Therefore, you can have victory over whatever it is you're dealing with. Even if there is no manifestation of happiness. Joy can be defined as:

➢ An inward evoking caused by well-being.

➢ Success, or good fortune.

➢ The prospect of possessing what one desires.

➢ A delightful expression and exhibition.

➢ Blissfulness and a source or a cause of delight.

God delights in your vindication. So, shout for joy and be glad. Because God will make even your enemies and those that revolt against you to stumble and fall. So that you will always say, "may the Lord be exalted, who has pleasure in the well-being of

His servant." Joy is listed as a fruit of the Spirit in Galatians 5:22 as well.

Therefore, lift-up your head and be glad. Don't dismay. Don't fear. Don't be sad. Because God has given you an everlasting abundance of happiness in the form of joy!

Happy Thought: Think of joy as an opportunity to trust God in the mist of opposition. Because joy conquers sadness. And joy is the revelation of everlasting happiness.

Happy Key Points to Remember:

➢ Happy people are the most joyful people to be around.

➢ Happy people are not easily worried.

➢ Stand for what is right and you will eventually be happy for not conforming to what you know is wrong.

➢ You must choose to be happy even when you're feeling sad.

➢ Happiness can be the outcome even in calamity.

➢ Joy is eternal, and happiness is a way of life.

➢ Joy conquers sadness.

Being Happy is the Goal!

VII

KNOW WHAT IT TAKES TO MAKE YOU HAPPY

Now days it seems as if everyone is looking for happiness: in people, places, and things. However, many lack core responsibilities to who they are in God and how God created them. Happiness is your responsible. And every human being is responsible for their own happiness. Yes, that's right. If you're an adult over 20 years or older. You are old enough to take full responsibility for your happiness.

Seems as though most people look to Hollywood and to entertainers as role models. Some look to people in general to show them the way to happiness, but only to be disappointed. Don't get me wrong everyone should have a role model and or mentor. However, you should never rely on another person as your soul source to achieving happiness.

Your happiness must come from within. And if people make you *"feel"* happy by what they say or do for you; that's a bonus towards your internal happiness. Because remember at any given time people can and will disappoint you. Therefore, you must know within your core being there lies the source of *all* happiness. You have within you the ability to make yourself happy. And it behooves you to find out what it takes to make you happy.

To be happy is the goal. Therefore, your heart must be soft and pliable for you to practice being happy and living a happy lifestyle. You must know your likes and your dislikes when it comes to knowing what it takes to make you happy. God has wired each and every one of us with the ability to house spiritual gifts. Gods Spirit within you is a power source that leads to happiness.

The greater one lives inside of you, if you have believed and received Him into your heart. The greater one is Jesus, who is the author and the finisher of our faith. There is nothing like knowing you have help to aide you to being happy. It's within you and it can only be activated by believing and trusting in God the Father, God the Son, and God the Holy Spirit.

You must know that no one or nothing can take the place of your happiness. No sickness, no disease, no lack, no corrupt communications, no other relationship. Nothing can steal your happiness or make you unhappy unless you let it. Do what it takes to make you happy and try not to seek happiness from outside sources such as in drugs (alcohol, opiates, prescription medications, etc.), material possessions, or people's affirmation of you. Also, learn to listen to your body and mind when it comes to doing what it takes to make you happy.

Try to eliminate stress and stressors. Your body will give you symptoms when you are carrying a heavy load of problems. Listen to your body and do what it takes to eliminate stress from out of your life. And don't let other people's problems become your drama.

The happy lifestyle is not necessarily a lifestyle of leisure. But, it's a lifestyle of discipline. And you may have to take inventory and eliminate clutter. There are some people and some things that can't go with you to your happy place.

Make a mental note that there are certain things happy people do, and certain ways happy people act. For instances, happy people are:

> Very humble and forgiving people. They choose to let go of offences.

> They are more prone to recognize when they are wrong and say they are sorry when they're wrong.

> They are not phony and they tend to be truly genuine, sincere, and honest.

> They hang around and network with other people that are positive and happy.

- They tend to make great leaders. Especially in leadership coaching.

- They tend to be less concerned about what others think about them. Whether its negative or positive comments a happy person is not moved either way or the other. Sure, they appreciate compliments and instructive criticism. But their whole state of being happy is not affect by what others say about them. In other words, they choose to be happy no matter what others may say about them.

- As a rule, happy people are not manipulators. They tend to be more influential and persuasive then controlling.

- Happy people tend to be more trust worthy. They also tend to be very transparent with nothing to hide. This is one of many reasons why they are so happy. Because the tend to not have to cover-up their true feelings.

- Happy people don't need a lot of "toys" or things so to speak to make them happy. Their happiness comes from within.

- Happy people have the keen ability to turn trials into triumph. And to turn problems into an opportunity.

- Happy people are focused on their goals and pursue their dreams easily.

- Happy people tend to have a more positive out-look on life.

- Happy people tend to make friends and acquaintances easily.

- Happy people are usually less likely to gossip, or be envious, and or jealous of others.

- Happy people are usually less likely to have low self-esteem.

- Happy people tend to be energetic and ambitious.

- Happy people tend to be adventurous.

- Happy people tend to adapt to change easily.

- Happy people take responsibility for their lives and the own up to their mistakes.

- Happy people are more likely to volunteer and lend a helping hand to others.

- Happy people are high achievers.

- Happy people are prone to laugh out loud and laugh often.

- Happy people tend to smile and greet others easily.

Happy Key Points to Remember:

➤ You must take full responsibility for your own happiness.

➤ You must know within your core being where your source of happiness comes from.

➤ To be happy is a goal.

➤ Nothing can steal your happiness or make you unhappy unless you let it.

➤ Do what it takes to make you happy and to be happy.

➤ The happy life is a lifestyle of discipline.

Happy Reflections

_____

_____

_____

_____

_____

_____

_____

_____

Happiness doesn't come in a bottle. And there is no magic to happiness. However, there is joy when you discover true happiness starts within you.

VIII

HOW BAD DO YOU WANT TO BE HAPPY?

Now that you know what it takes to make you happy. How bad do you want to be happy? Well let me warn you. Once you become happy and start living the happy lifestyle. You may become annoying to those who knew you when you were unhappy. And don't be surprised when you fully come into your happy place; negative and pessimistic people won't like being around you. Not because they don't like you per say. But it's because they resent the fact that you're living your life the way you want and that you are genuinely happy.

Don't get discouraged or offended at those that do not appreciate your happiness. Those that do not appreciate your happiness will begin to exit your life. Or your happiness will begin to rub off on them. And for those that remain negative and unhappy in your presence, be a positive force for them to reckon with. Because happiness is not free. It may cost you time, relationships, and decisions in order for you to be genuinely happy.

Happy Note: Once you become happy and start living the happy lifestyle. Some people that were used to hang around you, will not want to be around you anymore. Or you won't want to hang around them anymore. At first this may seem painful. However, it's too expensive for you to hang around bitter, angry, negative, and unhappy people. It'll cost you your happiness.

Although it may be necessary for you to change your circle of friends. You should never think more highly of yourself, than you ought. Because true happiness is never arrogant. And, there are some situations that you must pray through. For instance, I am not advocating you divorce your spouse just because you have differences. Or even if your spouse has a negative perspective on life. Some people you must pray through to get a break through. But remember it is *you* and not your spouse that has to adapt. Therefore, in situations like this. You have to exercise faith and patience until your spouse (and or children) grab hold of true happiness.

In most cases, you cannot change how people respond or react to you. Your circle of friends, associates, and even some family members, may or may not be attracted to your happiness. However, many will want to be in your company. Because they will be happy that you are happy.

Some people will say things like, "you changed", as though it's a bad thing. But I've already mentioned how the process to becoming happy can be rewarding and painful. Because most people feel uncomfortable with change. But once you truly grab hold and discover true happiness, it really doesn't matter what others think or say. Even if you make others feel uncomfortable. You must remember you are not a bad person because you disassociate yourself from negative people; whether friends, family, or foe.

There can be monetary cost associated with being happy as well. For instance, you may feel the need to take vacations or getaways. Or you may need to get a new hobby or do somethings you enjoy doing. Getting away and enjoying yourself can be refreshing. I highly recommend taking vacations and holidays away. Take time out for yourself and rest from all the pressures of life. Take a vacation out of the country or spending time on an Island in the Caribbean. Do whatever it takes. But always remember the choice is yours when it comes to your happiness, even if you don't get to take a vacation or a day off.

Happy Thought: There's no need to spend all your money or abandon your responsibilities when pursuing happiness. However, do what is necessary to eliminate the pressures and stressors of life. And when it comes to ensuring your happiness always remember to use wisdom and have a sense of balance.

Many people feel like death of a love one is a strain and drain on their happiness. And many often feel as if they can't be happy after a love one has died. Grieving the loss of a loved one can be hard and may be necessarily.

Even Jesus wept when his good friend Lazarus died. However, He got over His grievances. He did not hold on to grief for a long time. And of course, we know He did something about the situation, by raising Lazarus from the dead (See John 11). Nevertheless, even if you can't change your situation, you must always recognize the opportunity to move on. Because even in the mist of death. God can and will give you peace and joy in knowing that you can rest and rely on Him to help you through it.

We all grieve. However, it's too counterproductive for you to stay sad and grieved about something you can't change. Ask God to help you. And if you must, forgive yourself if you've done or said anything wrong to the person that has died. And you never got the chance to make things right with them. You must forgive yourself and move on. Because it'll cost you, your happiness.

God is well able to bring you through difficult situations in life. Therefore, don't get mad at yourself or God. But rejoice in the fact that God is for you and you can still have happiness in the mist of sorrow.

The process and timing of God is really, really something to consider when dealing with people, issues, situations, and the promises of God. And although the human intellect (the mind) can't phantom the ways of God in totality. You must always remember, Gods thoughts are not your thoughts, neither are His ways your ways (Isaiah 55:8). If God has promised you happiness and rest in the mist of troubles. Then you can rest assuredly that there is nothing to worry about.

Happy Note: The process to a happy lifestyle usually takes a series of actions or steps to achieve. And must be systematically planned out with continuous changes taking place. Happiness must also be carried out in a definite manner with a series of actions that bring about specific results towards being happy.

Up to this point, I have worked very hard and long in the pursuit of my own personal happiness. I want everything God has for me. Therefore, I am willing to pay the price. This should be your testimony as well. If you are a young person. I highly recommend that you do whatever it takes to secure your happiness. Pay the cost to be different and choose your friends wisely. Live to be happy within reason and moderation. And always do what is morally conducive to achieving happiness.

God is good and there are many promises in the bible concerning happiness. However, those big promises that you have been confessing and believing God for usually take time and you must go through a process. Timing is everything. For example, no good parent is going to give his or her son or daughter anything before his or her time. Or should I say before he or she can handle it. For instance, you wouldn't give a four-year-old child a Mercedes's Benz, would you? No, because you and I both know a four-year-old child cannot and should not be driving. You can promise the child one day that he or she will get a Mercedes. However, they still must wait and go through the *process* of growing up; taking a driver's training class; and passing the drivers training test before they can drive.

God is no different. You must mature before certain blessings and promises manifest in your life. You must also pass certain tests and trails to prove that you are ready to handle the blessings of God. Most importantly, you must never forget. It is God who blesses you, so you can enjoy *all* things richly. And so, the fruit of happiness can abound within you.

Therefore, you must always remain happy and confident until the blessings and the promises of God manifest in your life. And remember, God is not a man that He would lie (Numbers 23:19). If God promises you something, it will surely come to pass. And the process will be well worth the wait!

Happy Note: No matter how hard things may be. Remember God is for you and not against you. He wants you to be happy! (Reference Jerimiah 29:11).

Happy Key Points to Remember:

- ➤ It's too expensive for you to hang around bitter, angry, negative, unhappy people.

- ➤ It may be necessary for you to change your circle of friends and associates for you to be happy.

- ➤ Do what is necessary to eliminate anything that is costing you happiness.

- ➤ Don't divorce your spouse just because you have differences. Learn from each other and grow together.

- ➤ Even if you can't change your situation, you must be able to recognize the opportunity to move on.

- ➤ You can still have happiness even in the mist of grieving.

- ➤ Mature and pay the cost to be happy.

- ➤ Remain confident and happy until the blessings manifest in your life.

Happy Reflections

You can't control anyone's happiness; but you can control your happiness!

IX

HAPPY IS A LIFESTYLE

Remember how some fairy tale movies and stories end with happily ever-after endings? Well, I propose to you, the happy lifestyle is *not* a fairy tale. The happy lifestyle isn't a script that says, you must be perfect to be happy. Nor do you have to be happy all the time. You can obtain true happiness today, right now and forever. You don't have to wait until the end of the script. The happy lifestyle is obtainable and it can be a way of life, no matter what. You may need to get over certain situations and issues from the past. Get over whoever or whatever hurt you. Get over whoever took advantage of you. Get over whoever shamed your name, lied on you, mistreated you, abused you and said harmful things about you. Forgive and move on.

We all have had our share of negative things happen to us. There is not a person on this earth that doesn't have an enemy. Every person on the face of this earth will or has faced persecution, tests, trials, tribulations, and situations. But we mustn't let the enemy of our soul rob us of who we are and of our happiness.

Therefore, do not let bitterness and the *"oh woes me"* victim's mentality rob you from being happy!

Your happiness isn't predicated upon the actions of others. But upon your daily thoughts and actions. Therefore, you must exercise this power and right on a consistent basis. You're going to have to decide to live the happy lifestyle no matter what may come or what may go. Learn to be happy despite of what you may or may not have. Happiness that comes from God is a blessing. So, grab hold of it and tap into it daily.

Also make sure your heart and mind stays in peace during test and trials. Because murmuring and complaining only makes things worst. And note that most of the test and trails that we go through are *not* from God. However, He will use test and trials in hopes that you will trust Him and draw closer to Him. Most of the stuff you go through is either self-inflicted or brought on by the enemy of your soul. The devil is a master schemer and master planner at manipulating our minds into thinking that God is out to get us.

The devil is the accuser of the brethren. After he has caused calamities and distress in your life. Then he comes to taunt you with afflictions caused by stress. The devil, comes to steal, kill, and to destroy. And he is always on his job. But Jesus has said, He has come that you may have life and life more abundantly (John 10:10). Therefore, you must always be alert and on guard. Learn to live on the defense so you can live a happy and joyful life. Do not be ignorant of the devil's devises, lest you fall into his trap of depression and a state of no joy.

Recognize enemies come in many forms and fashions. The enemy can also be your subconscious mind and or your own divisive ways. We all have idiosyncratic tendencies that we possess. Therefore, recognize when you are in error. And try not to cover up or mask your mistakes. Confess and correct all wrongs if you can. And get right with people that you may have wronged. Make right choices and do not allow offenses from other people to hinder you. Even if someone may have done you wrong or caused you to walk in bitterness or unforgiveness. You must forgive them and get rid of all bitterness immediately. We'll talk more about bitterness and unforgiveness in Chapter 12.

Release all negativity. And always have a good defense against the negatives that are bound to happen in life. Draw close to God. And know whatever it is that you are going through it will come to pass. Learn to live the good life and walk in the fullness of joy and happiness. Practice being happy in all things. Because when you learn to react to situations differently and respond in a positive manner. Then you'll began to experience the happy (good) life. You'll also discover that you won't feel as depressed or anxious about situations.

Happy Note: As we get ready to embark upon the remaining chapters, I want you to prepare your hearts and minds. Get rid of all distractions and clutter, so you can make room for a happy lifestyle and journey. It's a great accomplishment to have joy in the face of difficulties and calamities. And remember it's not always about your problems as much as it is about your happiness.

Having balance in life is such a great asset. In most cases, a balanced person is usually more understanding, empathetic, and more positive than a person without balance. Having balance is a key element for every area of our lives. A balanced life will take you to greater heights and greater levels of happiness. Balance can be defined as:

> A state of equilibrium and the power and or the ability to influence, support, and or like the other side; To arrange, adjust, or proportion the parts of something to be equal or proportionate; and a state of thinking and realizing that different things have a proper amount of importance.

Sometimes people can get so out of balance in their thinking and obligations that they never ever reach the happy lifestyle. They don't do it intentionally. And most don't start off thinking we're going to be off balance, it just happens.

For instance, I can go months and months and months without watching television. Not to say this is a bad thing. Because this helps keep my mind clear of clutter and helps me to stay focused. However, there's a saying you can be so heavenly minded that you are no earthly good. Therefore, I've come to realize that I need other outlets and viewpoints to function in society. I also need to have different types of people around me with different perspectives. This helps keep me in a state of balance. Isn't this true for all of us? Because on the flip side. Some people all they do in their leisure time is listen to and watch things that are negative. Sometimes we just need a change of perspective to help us think more clearly and help us to be more balanced in life.

We all need people with a different perspective around us at some point or another. If it's not bad for you, nor causing you any harm. You should hang around people that don't look like you and think like you all the time. Hanging around people that look like you and think like you all the time, can cause you to become narrow minded and have in "the box" thinking, so to speak.

How are you ever going to learn something new if you don't explore different ethnicities, racial backgrounds, cultures, and lifestyles. The world is so big and with so many opportunities. Therefore, it is imperative that you learn all you can about other cultures and people as it relates to being happy.

This is one of the reasons why I believe social media and the internet is a wonderful tool, when used properly and when used in a balanced perspective. Different people from different backgrounds networking, sharing different opinions, ideals, and perspectives is a good thing. However, some of the information can be good and some not so good. Therefore, you must be selective what you entertain or research.

There's a lot of negative things on the internet that can frustrate and contaminate your state of happiness. Otherwise, the dialogues from different perspectives being shared via an open forum from people all over the world is a good thing.

Live the happy lifestyle on purpose. Practice working hard and playing hard. Don't be a person that only works all the time and never plays. This is out of balance. Your body and mind need to be revived, refreshed, rejuvenated, and renewed. As you learn to have a more balanced life in every area of your life, you'll begin to live the happy life!

Happy Note: There are classes that you can take to help relieve stress and help you have a more balanced life. I recommend good clean things like taking an exercise class, golfing, tennis, bible study, worship services, prayer and meditation, massage therapy, relaxations techniques, etc... Practice getting quiet and doing things that are clean and wholesome!

Happy Key Points to Remember:

➢ The happy lifestyle is not a fairy tale. It's Real!

➢ The happy lifestyle is obtainable and can be a way of life for you.

➢ Your happiness is going to be predicated upon your daily thoughts and actions.

➢ Learn to do away with anything that would cause you to walk around in bitterness.

➢ Having balance in life is such a great asset for a happy life.

➢ We all need people with a different perspective around us some of the time, so we can have a sense of happy balance in our lives.

➢ You must live the happy lifestyle on purpose.

X

HEALTH, HEALING &
HAPPINESS

Divine healing is available to all who believe in the miraculous healing power of God. However, what you eat, the amount of stress you have, and your emotional state of being all play a very important role in your overall health and wellness. Also, the manifestation of physical healing and wholeness in your mind, body, and soul is connected to your happiness.

There's a proverbial saying that says, "a merry heart doeth good like a medicine: but a broken spirit dries up the bones" (Proverbs 17:22). Therefore, health and healing can come from being happy. And from being full of joy, and laughter.

If you are able and you can, I recommend you laugh and laugh out loud often! However, if you know someone that is terminally ill and unable to laugh. Use wisdom. Because there are other ways to get the manifestation of healing to them. Pray for them. And play positive happy inspirational recordings and healing scriptures via CD, DVD, MP media, etc., where they lay. This is vital to their health and healing. Also have spiritual leadership and or elders of the local church to pray for them. This is vitally important as well.

A healthy mind, body, and soul is a happy mind, body, and soul. That's not to say that you won't have days that you don't feel like you are healed, happy, or whole.

If you are a woman, you must recognize the hormonal changes that they go through every month when they have their menstrual cycle. This can cause moodiness and irritability. Also recognize the changes the body goes through physiological during pre-menopause, menopause, and post-menopause. Hormonal changes can cause symptoms of depression, sadness, mood swings, unhappiness, etc., ... Therefore, it is imperative that both men and women know their body.

Medical doctors and psychologist say laughter releases healing endorphins. And there are several different ways to get a good release and an effective happy laugh by:

➤ Listening to and watching clean wholesome comedians, that are funny and entertaining in a good and positive why.

➤ Try to smile and smile often while thinking about the good things in life.

➤ Enjoy your children and grandchildren while their young. Children are fun, funny, and can make you laugh easily.

- Don't sweat the small things. Nor worry about everything. Learn to let go and release people, places, and situations that affect your happiness.

- Learn to get cozy and relaxed. This will help your mind and body heal and will prepare you to be comfortable with laughing as you relax.

- Get rid of excessiveness. Organize your life and learn to release clutter.

- Instead of being stressed and uptight: think, think, think happy thoughts. Because your mind will try to convince you that there are 110 negative things to think about, instead of thinking heathy positive thoughts.

Your overall wellbeing is tied to your physiological and genealogical makeup. Take good care of yourself and watch what you eat. Because your body is your temple. Therefore, eat healthy, exercising, and go on a healthy detox diet every so often. This is a great way to start a happy healthy lifestyle. There are many nutritionists, healthy lifestyle doctors, and board-certified physicians that are trained in nutritional therapy, homeopathy, and detoxification. Do your research on dietary practices that are geared towards getting you to eating healthy and feeling happier.

Keep your mind healthy with whole thoughts, throughout the day. Also, learn to reject and denounce any negative words that you have spoken over yourself. As well as negative words and connotations spoken over you by other people. Again, there's nothing like laughter. And if you take the time to live and laugh. You'll find peace, happiness, health, and healing for your mind, body, and soul.

Your health and healing mean's everything as far as your happiness is concerned. Your psychological and physiological wellbeing is more important than money. What good is money without being healthy, happy, and whole to enjoy it.

Some people tend to take more care of their houses, homes, cars, and pets than themselves. This should not be. Your health is everything. And what you put in your body as well as what products you put on your body is very important. Read ingredient labels and learn to eat healthy. And practice using healthy and natural hair and skin care products as well.

Learning to be happy with how you look is important to your wellbeing as well. Your physical appearance has a lot to do with your state of mind and wholeness. Learn to love your body and love the way God has created you.

As a former cosmetologist, I know how important this is. I've learned that beauty and grooming is very important to health and wholeness. Having your hair groomed and physical body groomed can be refreshing and healthy. Groomed hair has a tremendous impact on how you feel. Shower and bathe daily.

There's nothing like bathing in water daily. Water is cleansing and water is therapeutic and refreshing.

Dress appropriately and wear what makes you feel good and comfortable. Dress in clean modest attire. Your attire and the way you dress; and the clothes you wear says a lot about who you are and how you feel about yourself. Dress for success even if you're a stay-at-home mom or a business man working from home. Color coordination is important. Dark colors are good for fall and winter. And brighter colors are good to wear during spring and summer seasons. However, wear what makes you happy! Because different colors and different styles look different on different people.

There's a saying, "beauty is in the eyes of the beholder". Therefore, learn to possess inner beauty. Inner beauty that radiates from the inside out. And if you're a man this goes for you as well. Be handsome and valiant both inside and outside. Put your best "foot" forward. Always expressing a healthy happy you.

Happy Key Points to Remember:

➢ The manifestation of physical healing and wholeness in your body is connected to your happiness.

➢ Laugh and laugh out loud often!

➢ Your happiness is vital to you being well.

➢ Health and healing are everything when it comes to your happiness.

➢ Eating healthy is a great way to start a happy healthy lifestyle.

➢ Your psychological and physiological health is more important than money.

➢ Keep your mind healthy and whole throughout the day.

➢ Learn to reject and denounce any negative words that have been spoke over you.

➢ Your health, happiness and overall wellbeing is also tied to your attitude and thinking.

XI

LOVE & HAPPINESS

Whether in marriage, business, or friendship one must understand the concept of love and happiness. This chapter will help you understand and maintain a sense of happiness regardless if your relationships *make* you happy or not. The knowledge needed here is so you can mature and be able to understand how relationships work and so you won't be in a state of confusion. Or in a perpetual state of rude awakenings when it comes to love and happiness.

The divorce rate and the breakup of the family in America is outstanding. I believe it's because people are entering marriage hoping their spouse will *make* them happy. And although having love in your life can equate to happiness. However, a good deal of people, fail to realize that their spouse is not their sole source to making them happy. The sooner we learn this the better we can appreciate the marriage relationship and relationships in general.

Knowing and appreciating the fact that marriage is for fellowship, companionship, fruitfulness, purpose multiplication, and for aiding and sharing common interest will help in the overall understanding of what marriage is for. Therefore, if your mate makes you happy then that's an added benefit to the covenant relationship of marriage. A bonus or gratuity within the confounds of the relationship. Because most marriages form from a place of love, fellowship, companionship. And some for security, therefore, not necessarily for happiness *alone*.

Remember the song from the seventies, *"Love and Happiness"* sung by singer Al Green? Well that song gave us the concept of how love and happiness should go hand and hand. Love is divine. And love is more than just a feeling. Matter of fact, love means a lot more than happiness, such as:

- to hold dear.
- to cherish, to care for.
- to feel passion, devotion, or tenderness for.
- to like or desire actively and take pleasure in.
- to feel strong affection or experience intense desire for.

Therefore, one must hold dear to love as you pursue the happy life. Love and happiness can go hand and hand. However, you must always remember and understand that your happiness is not based on whether you're loved, in love, or not. Nor is it based on having or being in a physical relationship.

Having a loving relationship in your life and being happily married can be a wonderful thing. But remember just because you're in a "relationship" doesn't automatically mean happiness *all* the time. Your happiness should not be based upon your feelings. Neither should your happiness be based upon another person. Having a person to comfort you and make you feel good is great. But love and happiness should never be predicated upon comfort. Because what if you're the one always giving the love and comfort and the other person doesn't in return?

Every human being was created to love and to be loved. And whether you know it or not, we learn early in life that love is a necessity. However, some people think love is just having fun, talking kind, warm, cute, cuddly words. But love is more than telling someone you love them and having fun together. Love is doing things for others even when you don't want to. Love is more than coming together and having fun together. However, love can lead to happiness. But the question still remains... what if it doesn't?

The bible says, David the King of Jerusalem, encouraged himself, when he was in an uncomfortable situation (1 Samuel 30:6). Therefore, you must always remember to encourage yourself whenever you find yourself unhappy or not being loved in return.

Sometimes loving others can be difficult and can hurt. Therefore, as I keep reiterating throughout this book. Your happiness is a choice! You must choose to be happy in love or out of love. And if you are in a caring loving relationship. Then kudos for you. I pray you will be happy always.

When you begin to recognize and know the difference between real love and happiness. Then life circumstances *can't* alter true love and happiness in your life. So often people mistake sexuality and sex with love. And those that are more prone to sexual promiscuity; sometimes tend to think sex is the ultimate destiny to happiness. When in fact it could just be a pleasurable moment that ends in disaster. This can be a problem. Because there are some people that can have sex and not necessarily love the other person.

Sex and love are not the same. And those that equate sex outside of marriage, often end up hurt in most cases. Love should never be equated to a mere physical feeling or attraction. Being in love should lead to a loving committed marriage.

When people meet for the first time. Or go out on a date for the first time. There can be great chemistry and the two can get along fine. However, one day and believe me that one day is sure to come. If they continue to date and hang around each other, they are bound to eventually disagree about something.

When dating for any significate amount of time you'll discover that there are somethings that you both do not like about each another. Or somethings you might see differently. Or somethings the other person does not make you feel good or happy about. And if you stay in a relationship long enough with any person, they are sure to get on your nerves and vice versus.

Relationships can be very rewarding and very difficult at the same time. Because most relationships cause for a degree of tolerance in order for them to work and function properly. Whether it's a working relationship, a friendship, or a committed engagement, or marriage. You must cultivate and cherish your relationships.

Friendship is one of the most important aspects of any relationship. You must become friends first before you can trust one another. It takes time to get to know one another. If you don't take time to get to know one another's likes and dislikes. Then love and happiness within the relationship won't be perfected and the relationship can easily be fragmented.

Happy Note: The more you know about a person the more you trust them; the greater your love will be towards them. And hopefully the happier the two of you will be.

If you are single and by yourself for now. Don't wait for another person to come along to be happy. Now is the time to be happy. Today is your day to be happy. There are so many things that one can do to be fulfilled and happy. While your single you might find fulfilment in helping others. People that are least fortunate. And if you are single one of the best things you can do is fulfil your destiny and purpose in life without distraction, until someone comes along. Love is an action word. Therefore, learn to give back to yourself and others in your season of singleness.

Happy Note: Love is the key if you're ever going to be happy. Love yourself and others even if you are single. Make giving love and receiving love your state of being.

Those of you that are caregivers. I pray you will help others in the spirit of love and serve others with joy. By sharing and showing love to others even if they don't appreciate it. This is not to say most people are unappreciative. It's just the opposite. Most people are happy to have someone love and care for them. However, there's a few people that may never appreciate what you do for them. But that's not to say you should be *unhappy*. Keep sowing love and you shall reap love.

Being alone and loneliness is not the same. Being alone means you are single or have singleness of mind; and single and or separated from others for a moment in time. However, loneliness means being without company or cut off from others. Desolate and or *not* frequented by human beings. Loneliness often causes people to become depressed and sad. This is especially true for the elderly. And this can be a problem for some when it comes to love and happiness.

Each one of us is different. And if you ever want to be successful being happy then you must understand people can be fickle. Be prepared to deal with people in a proper perspective as it relates to love and happiness. People can sometimes make you feel good, love you, and hate you all at the same time. But this should not affect your happiness. Because as we discussed previously and as I keep reiterating. Happiness is not predicated upon feelings nor upon someone else trying to make you happy.

Relationships are work in general. Therefore, don't think everyone you encounter wants to be your friend or even like you for that matter. And if you're the type of person that is always looking for people to like you. I hate to say it. You are in for a rude awaking and for serious heart ache. Not everyone is going to like you. I always like to say, "people are people"! Meaning just that. People are not God, nor do they have the capacity to love you like God can. Nor do they have the power to make feel happy or keep you happy all the time. So, stop depending on people for your happiness. And learn to love yourself and pursue the happiness within you.

Happy Key Points to Remember:

➢ Your spouse isn't in your life to *make* you happy.

➢ Your relationships are for many reasons other than or just for happiness.

➢ You must hold dear to love as you pursue the happy lifestyle.

➢ Recognize and know the difference between real love and happiness.

➢ Relationships cause for tolerance and lots of love in order for them to function properly.

➢ You must be prepared to deal with people in a proper perspective as it relates to love and happiness.

➢ There are so many things that you can do to be fulfilled and happy.

➢ Be prepared to deal with people in a proper perspective as it relates to love and happiness.

Happy Reflections

Don't Get Bitter! Get Better!

XII

HINDRANCES TO HAPPINESS

I saved this chapter for last. Because I really don't want you to forget how important it is to be happy and to stay happy for the rest of your life. If your heart is not bitter or hardened, but soft and pliable. Then you are susceptible to being happy when everyone and everything around you may be going crazy, mad, sad, angry, and disgusted.

Look at society, today! And you'll notice people are doing a lot of things or saying a lot of things in direct correlation to their own bitterness, anger, and sadness. People are angry for a host of reasons. Some because of past hurts and disappointments. Others because of what someone has done to them or hasn't done for them. All while knowing, what's done in the past is history.

Forgiveness is everything and walking in forgiveness has everything to do with your future happiness. Even if you feel like you don't like a person for whatever reason. You must learn to forgive them if you are ever going to be happy. Even if someone has offended you. You may feel like you don't want to be in their presence or have anything to do with them. That's okay, fine. Because you don't have to subject yourself to abuse, persecution., or cruelty. However, if you're ever going to be happy, then you must make it your priority and your duty to walk in forgiveness and to walk in love.

Real forgiveness is when you look at person and say within yourself, "I forgive them, because they know not what they do". Offenses can be turned into opportunities for your good. Stepping stones for you to learn something about your character and for you to grow. If you began to look at problems as opportunities, then all things will begin to work together for your good. When you learn to forgive those that you consider have "wronged" you. And consider loving people and stop hating people for whatever reason. Then and only then will your life begin to heal and take on a new level of happiness.

Happy Note: Being happy doesn't mean you should smile all the time or feel good all the time. However, being happy is a condition of the heart. If your heart is conditioned in such a way that you are forgiving and can let go of offenses. Then you can live a happy life without hindrance.

Let's take a look at the story of Joseph in the bible. The story begins in the book of Genesis with Joseph's life and his family's legacy. Joseph was his father's favorite child and was hated by his brothers because of it. His very own brothers were jealousy and had a zeal to kill him. However, instead of killing him. They chose to sell him into slavery. After which Joseph had every right to be bitter, hard heartened, and angry at his brothers. But Joseph turned his tragedy into purpose. He was forced to trust God with his life because of the situation. As it turned out, what Josephs brothers meant for evil, God worked it out for Joseph's *good and wellbeing*. Joseph eventually became prime minister of Egypt, the land in which he was sold into. He was also able to save all of Egypt, his family, and brothers from a devastating famine (See Genesis 37, 39, 40-45).

Happy Note: Happiness is when you are hurting but you choose to look at your problems as opportunities. This is not to say that we should not be concerned about our problems. Nor does it exemplify the fact that we should not deny that we have hurts or problems. However, if we choose to trust God and let all things work together for our good. Then we shall be happy. Because we trust God and we realize He is in control.

Like Joseph, most people have been through some very challenging things in life, especially when it comes to dealing with family or those closest to us. But when we learn every situation has a purpose or there's an opportunity attached to it. Then we can choose to not be depressed and choose to be happy. In most cases problems become things of the past. And with the experience you've gained. You'll be able to help someone else through their difficulties. So instead of choosing to be sad, mad, and depressed. Learn to be happy.

Unforgiveness is a major, major happiness blocker. Many people that are unhappy today is because they are harboring unforgiveness in their hearts. I truly believe every person on this earth has a reason to be justified in being offended and or unforgiving. However, just because someone offends you, God still wants you to walk in love. So, you'll be able to inherit the blessings that He has for you.

Unforgiveness is like cancer. It eats away at you until it consumes you. It's also like poison. It's toxic, and it is designed to kill the person that is unforgiving. The sin of unforgiveness puts many people on the path to darkness. But if God can forgive you of all your deepest darkest sins. Then you ought to be willing to forgive others of their sins, offenses, or whatever it is they have done to you.

I have a saying that I like to say, and it goes like this, "love the sinner, but hate the sin". Therefore, be quick and willing to forgive others. The things people do to us or against us, must be forgiven. Because most of the time hurting people hurt people and most of the time, they know not what they do.

Happy Note: God will use what someone has done to you as a stepping stool to bigger and greater things. God will use everything that you have been through in life as a lesson and as a testimony.

In the book of Matthew 18:21-22, Peter came to Jesus and said, "Lord, how many times may my brother sin against me and I forgive him? Up to seven times?" Jesus said to him, "I tell you, not seven times but seventy times seven!" Therefore, forgive others even if they are wrong and you are right.

Forgiveness doesn't mean you must hang around the person that has offended you. Nor does it mean you should build a relationship with them. But you must be careful not to allow un-forgiveness to hinder your happiness. Don't allow unforgiveness to swell so big in your heart that it blocks you from loving people. And most importantly don't allow un-forgiveness to block your blessings!

The fruit of unforgiveness is:

➤ Bitterness
➤ Sickness
➤ Disease
➤ Hatred
➤ Jealousy
➤ Death

The fruit of forgiveness is:

➤ Love

- Happiness
- Joy
- Peace
- Prosperity
- Healthy
- Wealth
- Wholeness
- Blessings

Forgiveness is necessary for your success and for you to be happy in every area of your life. Because as sure as the sun rises in the East. The enemy *(the devil)* will use someone or something to cause you to walk in unforgiveness. The enemy comes to steal, kill, and to destroy happiness. He comes to get you off track from your destiny to being happy and to living a fulfilling happy life.

Therefore, learn to forgive so you can be forgiven. Forgive and forget, if you can. Let go and let God! God is well able to forgive you and heal you from your past mistakes and from the wounds of others! God loves you and His mercy is sufficient for you. So be healed, happy, and whole.

Happy Note: offense is another hindrance to your happiness. You can't control anyone else's behavior. However, you can control how you respond to offenders. Don't let being offended at

another person cause you to walk in strife and discontentment.
You can choose to be happy.

Bitterness can also be a hindrance to your happiness. Therefore, choose to be happy and not bitter. Start each day saying, "I am happy". Get on social media and post, "I am happy"! Be grateful for the little things in life. These are just some of the things I did when I was going through difficult times.

I'd get on social media and post "I'm happy"! And before I knew it. I started to *"feel"* happy. All the while no one knew what I was going through. And before long *"I am happy"* became my favorite saying. Just like most people I've had my share of suffering and hurts. We all go through difficult situations. But I'd post it and say it anyways. *"I am Happy"*! And the more I said it, the more I became happy! And to this day my confession remains, "I am happy"!

Choosing to be happy is what a mature person does. I remember in my younger years, when I use to have problems and or situations. I used to get on the phone and call everyone I could think of, that would listen to my sad situation or ordeal. I'd tell them all about my dilemma. I spent countless years doing this and in most cases the person on the other end of the phone had just as many problems and or issues that I had. They could not help me. At best all they could do is pray for me.

Having someone listen to your problems can sometimes help and I highly recommend counseling if needed. However, sharing and talking about your problems with another person is not necessarily a solution. There should come a time in your life when you stop relying on people to help you be comfortable and happy.

Likewise, I've learned in every situation to give thanks. Because there is not one person on this earth that has not gone through trauma. Not one person on this planet, born of many days is *without* trouble. When you learn to look at adversity and problems and say, "I choose to be happy". Then you are on the road to living a happy lifestyle despite what you may or may not go through.

Try not to hang around negative people who gossip and backbite. Gossip and backbiting will hinder you from happiness. Negativity and gossip can be very subtle. Especially, when it's coming from a friend and or love one. If your anything like me, you want to help people and support people. But somethings are just not worth your happiness.

If you continue to hang around people who refuse to change and who continue to dump negativity on you. Then I can guarantee you will become grieved in your spirit. This can cause you to become bitter, negative, and unhappy if you're not careful. I recommend, you separate yourself from bitter and negative people. I hate to say this, but I don't care if the person is a family member.

Separation is sometimes necessary for your health, peace, and happiness.

Husbands and wives this may not apply to you. Because marriage is a *holy* covenant and sacrament and should be honored for better or for worst. I recommend you pray and ask God to help you, if your spouse is negative and critical. God may or may not change them. However, He will change you. He'll give you the patience to bare it and the grace to love them in spite of their behavior. And in return they'll see your happiness and it may provoke them to change for the better.

Now days there are so many things that can cause a person to become unhappy and bitter. For example, anxiety and mental health disorders are characterized by feelings of worry. Anxiety and fear are feelings that can be strong enough to interfere with one's daily activities. Things such as:

- Stress
- Worry
- Gossip
- Eating Disorders
- Being Overweight
- Over Spending
- Negativity
- The Victims Mentality
- Use of Recreational Drugs

> Health Issues

All these can cause a person to become off balanced and unhappy. There are many things that can hinder your happiness. But the reality is no one thing or no one should have that much power over your life! Even in the mist of living in a world that is forever evolving and changing. We must keep our minds focused on the positive. Put this into practice every day and learn to do good. Strive to live a life of excellence, harmony, peace, joy, and happiness with everybody.

Stay focused by keeping your mind focused. Because an unfocused mind can put you at odds with others and yourself. Learn to mimic people that are happy and living a positive happy lifestyle. Hang around people that are comfortable with their inner self. People that are happy tend to be a positive force to be around and to emulate. They tend to be happy in their work, with their loved ones, and with themselves. Even in the mist of distractions.

A distraction can be anything that hinders your happiness. A distraction can also be anything that prevents you from giving your full attention to what's important in your life. Distractions usually come in the form of *busyness*. Busyness that prevents you from moving forward and to your next level in life. Distraction is also the process of diverting your attention from your desired goals in life. Thereby blocking and or diminishing your happiness.

Distraction can be many things, many situations, and sometimes people. Distractions are often caused by:

> The lack and ability to pay attention
> Lack of interest
> The great intensity, novelty or attractiveness of something other than the goal and or promise
> Diversion
> Interruption
> Disturbance
> Interference
> Drama
> Extreme agitation of the mind or emotions often caused by strife, offense and or lust for something that is intended to take one off course.

What does the Bible say about distractions as it pertains to happiness? Romans 12:2 says, "Do not be conformed to this world, but be transformed by the renewal of your mind, that by testing you may discern what is the will of God, what is good and acceptable and perfect". You see, the enemy of your soul seeks to distract you in any way possible. His goal is to keep you in a state of distraction, confusion, and uncertainty. Therefore, robbing you of happiness.

1 Peter 5:8 says, "be sober, be vigilant; because your adversary the devil, as a roaring lion, walks about, seeking whom he may devour". However, James 4:7 says, submit to God, resist the devil and he will flee from you.

Sometimes we must stop everything and get in a quiet place to hear from God. Mark 6:31 says,

> Then Jesus said, "Let's go off by ourselves to a
> quiet place and rest awhile." He said this because
> there were so many people coming and going that
> Jesus and his apostles didn't even have time to eat.

We must prioritize our time. There must be a time for prayer daily. Ephesians 5:15-16 says:

> So, then, be careful how you live. Do not be unwise
> but wise, making the best use of your time because
> the times are evil.

Mark 1:35 states that Jesus, "in the morning, rising a great while before day, he went out, and departed into a solitary place, and there prayed".

Being distracted by the cares of life will cause you to go into a state of depression if you let it. Matthew 6:31-33, says, don't ever worry what you're going to eat; or what are we going to drink; or what are we going to wear. Because it is the unbelievers who are eager for all these things. Surely your heavenly Father knows what you have need of! Therefore, seek ye first the kingdom of God and his righteousness, and all these things will be provided for you as well.

Doing too many things and getting distracted can cause you to stop spending time with God in prayer and meditation. Therefore, you must never let others distract you from spending time with God and meditating on His promises in the Bible. Galatians 1:10 states,

> am I now trying to win the approval of human beings, or of God? Or am I trying to please people? If I were still trying to please people, I would not be a servant of Christ.

Bottom-line is don't allow anything to hinder your happiness in God. Also, don't allow the blessing blocker of offense, unforgiveness, bitterness, strife, and distraction swell big in your thoughts, emotions, and life. That it hinders you from your blessings!

Happy Thought: As we close this chapter your homework is to get rid of all distraction and clutter in your heart, your mind and your environment, so you can make room for the happy lifestyle.

Happy Key Points to Remember:

➤ Being happy is a condition of the heart.

➤ If you're going to be happy then you're going to have to make it a priority to walk in forgiveness.

➤ Happiness is when you are hurting but you choose to laugh at your problems and help others.

➤ Bitterness can be a hindrance to your happiness.

➤ Gossip and backbiting will rob you of happiness.

➤ Doing too many things and getting distracted can cause you to miss out on happiness and what God has for you.

Happy Thoughts

Happiness is true success!

EPILOGUE

I hope you've enjoyed reading each chapter and learning about the happy lifestyle. However, I guarantee you won't be able to remember everything you've read. Therefore, this book should be read, marked, tabbed, and read again and again. Keep this book as a reference whenever, you find yourself in a dilemma and or situation that compromises your happiness. I am certain that you will be able to use the teachings and the revelation that was unveiled for the rest of your life.

Began to journal and make mental notes of your progress. Always have a conscientious awareness of being happy. This book is an excellent resource to your happiness. And although it's not meant to be a quick fix to every situation. You should notice growth and progress towards being happy despite adversity.

Always remember your happiness isn't predicated upon another person making you happy. And after reading this book I hope you will never ever depend on anything or anyone to make you happy again. Practice being happy even if you are the sole source of your happiness. There is joy inside of you. More than you know.

Also keep in mind you. You must take time to put into practice what you've learned. Because action speaks louder than words; and faith without works is ineffective. Speaking and thinking happy thoughts when you feel sad is also required of you. Then and only then will you discover being happy is a wonderful and joyful experience. A happy you, means a happy future and a happy life. And don't forget to take the time to also study the scriptures found in Appendix II. And speak them out loud and frequently. As well as the declarations and affirmations found in Appendix I.

There is no other life to live than to be happy. Everybody wants to be happy. Therefore, it is required of you to share this book and share what you have learned. Share, share, share. Because the happier people are, the more-happy people we'll have in the earth. And this will be better for us all.

Happiness is the goal. And remember when things go wrong, and your mind tells you to believe and think the worst. That's the time to make the decision to choose to be happy. Remember the choice is yours. And truth be told, a happy person is a grateful person who chooses to be happy because they know things could be a lot worst. It is my prayer that this book will revolutionize your life and cause you to be happy for the rest of your life.

Don't forget to Laugh and Laugh out Loud Often!

Declare Today and Say Out Loud:
I Choose to Be Happy!

APPENDIX I

HAPPY DECLARATIONS & AFFIRMATIONS

- ➢ I decree and declare happy is my lifestyle.

- ➢ I'm happy and I don't care who doesn't like it.

- ➢ I will not let someone else's drama ruin my happiness.

- ➢ Learn to laugh even with sadness in your heart and tears rolling down your face.

- ➢ Learn to laugh out loud and often.

- ➢ Victory is being happy and staying happy.

- ➢ It's the little things in life make me happy.

- ➢ Happiness comes from within and it can't be bought.

- ➢ Life is happy when I trust in God.

- ➢ Every day is a blessed day when your living life on purpose.

- ➢ I have joy and happiness in all I do.

- ➢ I'm happy despite what I may be going through.

- I may not have everything I want or need, but I'm happy.

- I wake up every day thinking happy thoughts.

- I will not seek happiness from outside sources or possessions.

- I choose to eliminate all clutter, people, and things that hinder me from the pursuit of happiness.

- Nothing or no one has the capacity to make me happy within.

- I choose to be happy.

- I refuse to let anyone, or anything steal my joy (happiness).

- I receive happiness in my heart today.

- The joy of the Lord is my strength.

- I'm happy despite what I may or may not have.

- I'm happy and positive every day.

- I'm happy even when I should be sad.

- I'm happy helping others.

- I'm happy and at rest in the most difficult situations.

- Happy is the only way I live.

- I'm going to be happy no matter what.

Happiness is ....

APPENDIX II

HAPPY SCRIPTURES

1 Kings 10:8	*Happy* are thy men, happy are thy servants, which stand continually before thee, and that hear thy wisdom.
2 Chronicles 9:7	*Happy* are thy men, and happy are thy servants, which stand continually before thee, and hear thy wisdom.
Psalms 144:15	*Happy* is that people, that is in such a case: yea, *happy* is that people, whose God is the Lord.
Psalms 146:5	*Happy* is he that hath the God of Jacob for his help, whose hope is in the Lord his God.
James 5:11	Behold, we count them *happy* which endure. Ye have heard of the patience of Job and have seen the end of the Lord; that the Lord is very pitiful, and of tender mercy.

Proverbs 16:20	He that handles a matter wisely shall find good: and whoso trust is in the Lord, *happy* is he.
John 13:17	If ye know these things, *happy* are ye if ye do them.
Proverbs 3:13	*Happy* is the man that finds wisdom, that gets understanding.
Proverbs 3:18	She is a tree of life to them that lay hold upon her: and *happy* is every one that retains her.
Proverbs 29:18	Where there is no vision, the people perish: but he that keeps the law, *Happy* is he.
Jeremiah 12:1	Righteous art thou, O Lord, when I plead with thee: yet let me talk with thee of thy judgments: Wherefore doth the way of the wicked prosper? Wherefore are all they *happy* that deal very treacherously?
Genesis 30:13	And Leah said, *Happy* am I, for the daughters will call me blessed: and she called his name Asher.

Job 5:17	Behold, *happy* is the man whom God corrects: therefore, despise not thou the chastening of the Almighty.
Proverbs 14:21	He that despises his neighbor sins: but he that hath mercy on the poor, *Happy* is he.
Proverbs 28:14	*Happy* is the man that fears the Lord always: but he that hardens his heart shall fall into mischief.
1 Peter 3:14	But if ye suffer for righteousness' sake, *happy* are you: and be not afraid of their terror neither be troubled.
Deut. 33:29	Happy art thou, O Israel: who is like unto thee, O people saved by the Lord, the shield of thy help, and who is the sword of thy Excellency! And thine enemies shall be found liars unto thee; and thou shalt tread upon their high places.
Psalms 127:5	*Happy* is the man that hath his quiver full of them: they shall not be ashamed, but they shall speak with the enemies in the gate.

Romans 14:22	Hast thou faith? Have it to thyself before God. *Happy* is he that condemns not himself in that thing which he allowed.
Chronicles 9:7	How *happy* your people must be! How happy your officials, who continually stand before you and hear your wisdom.
John 16:33	These things I have spoken unto you, that in me ye might have peace. In the world ye shall have tribulation: but be of good cheer; I have overcome the world.
Revelation 21:4	And God shall wipe away all tears from their eyes; and there shall be no more death, neither sorrow, nor crying, neither shall there be any more pain: for the former things are passed away.
1 Thess. 5:16-18	Rejoice evermore. Pray without ceasing. In everything give thanks: for this is the will of God in Christ Jesus concerning you.
Philippians 4:4	Rejoice in the Lord always and again I say, Rejoice.
Nehemiah 8:10	Then he said unto them, go your way, eat the fat, and drink the sweet, and send

portions unto them for whom nothing is prepared: for this day is holy unto our Lord: neither be ye sorry; for the joy of the Lord is your strength.

Job 8:21   God will yet fill your mouth with laughter and your lips with shouts of joy.

Psalms 30:5   Weeping may endure for a night, but joy cometh in the morning.

Psalm 118:24   This is the day which the Lord hath made; we will rejoice and be glad in it.

Isaiah 12:3   With joy you will draw water from the wells of salvation.

John 15:11   These things have I spoken unto you, that my joy might remain in you, and that your joy might be full.

Romans 12:12   Rejoicing in hope; patient in tribulation; continuing instant in prayer.

Psalms 118:24   This *is* the day *which* the Lord hath made; we will rejoice and be glad in it.

Habakkuk 3:18   Yet I will rejoice in the Lord, I will joy in the God of my salvation.

Let happiness define you!

GLOSSARY

Adversity   a state or instance of serious or continued difficulty or misfortune

Affirmation   the act of affirming: something affirmed: a positive assertion

Authentic   not false or imitation: real, actual, authentic and true to one's own personality: spirit or character is sincere and authentic with no pretensions

Balance   a means of judging or deciding: stability: mental and emotional steadiness

Bitterness   being relentlessly determined: vehement: exhibiting intense animosity: harshly reproachful marked by cynicism and rancor: intensely unpleasant especially in coldness or rawness

Blessings   the act or words of one that blesses: blessing, approval, encouragement: a thing conducive to happiness or welfare: grace

Declaration   a formal or explicit announcement: the act of making an official statement about something: the act of declaring something: something that is stated or made known in an official or public way

Decree	call, command, dictate, direct, mandate, ordain, order
Destiny	something to which a person or thing is destined: a predetermined course of events often held to be an irresistible power for the future
Disease	a change in a person that prevents them from functioning normally: sickness or illness that affects a person: a condition that prevents the body or mind from working normally
Distraction	the act of distracting the state of being: diversion of attention, mental confusion: driven to distraction by something that distracts: an object that directs one's attention away from something else: confusion of thoughts or feelings
Famous	widely known: honored for achievement: very well-known
Feelings	generalized bodily consciousness, sensation, or responsive awareness: an emotional state or reaction: susceptibility to impression: identifiable sensation, perception, or thought: the overall quality of one's awareness: conscious recognition

Forgiveness   the act of forgiving someone or something: the attitude of someone who is willing to forgive other people: the act of ending anger at

Genuine   sincerely and honestly felt or experienced: actual, true, authentic, genuine, bona fide, actual, exactly: implies being fully trustworthy as according with fact: not fake or false

Goals   the end toward which an effort is directed

Happiness   a state of well-being and contentment: joy, joyful, pleasurable, or satisfying experience

Healing   to make free from injury or disease: to make sound or whole: heal a wound to make well again: to restore to health

Hindrances   a person or thing that makes a situation difficult: a person or thing that hinders someone or something: the act of making it difficult for someone to act or for something to be done: the act of hindering someone or something

Joy   to experience great pleasure or delight: a feeling of great happiness: a source or cause of great happiness: something or someone that gives joy to someone: success in doing, finding, or getting something

Lifestyle   a way of living: the way a person lives or a group of people live

Love   to hold dear: to cherish: to feel passion, devotion, or tenderness for: to like or desire actively: take pleasure in: to feel affection or experience desire

Negative   harmful or bad: not wanted: thinking about the bad qualities of someone or something: thinking that a bad result will happen: not hopeful or optimistic: expressing dislike or disapproval

Peace   a quiet and calm state of mind: agreement and harmony among people: a state of tranquility: freedom from disquieting or oppressive thoughts or emotions: harmony in personal relations

Practice   to do something again and again to become better at it: to do (something) regularly or constantly as an ordinary part of your life: to live according to the customs and teachings of

Prosperity   the condition of being successful or thriving; especially: economic well-being

Positive	good or useful: thinking about the good qualities of someone or something: thinking that a good result will happen: hopeful or optimistic: completely certain or sure that something is correct or true
Purpose	the reason why something is done or used: the aim or intention of something: the feeling of being determined to do or achieve something: the aim or goal of a person
Rich	having a lot of money and possessions: very expensive and beautiful, impressive, etc.: having or supplying a large amount of something that is wanted or needed.
Sickness	unhealthy condition of body or mind: the state of being sick: a specific type of disease or illness.
Stress	a state of mental tension and worry caused by problems in your life, work, etc.: something that causes strong feelings of worry or anxiety: physical force or pressure.
Test	to use a set of questions or problems to measure someone's skills, knowledge, or abilities: a set of questions or problems by which a person's knowledge, intelligence, or skills are measured: a critical examination, observation, or evaluation.

Trials   to be heavy, or weary: plod, trudge: do poorly in
                  relation to others.

Tribulations   distress or suffering resulting from oppression or
                  persecution; also: a trying experience: unhappiness,
                  pain, or suffering: an experience that causes
                  someone to suffer

ABOUT THE AUTHOR

Christine is an ordained minister who frequently speaks out on being blessed and the happy lifestyle! She enjoys coaching people how to live a happy and prosperous life. It is her desire to be a blessing to those she comes in contact with.

She is the author and publisher of several books. And she has earned several degrees: Bachelor of Arts (University Detroit Mercy - Detroit, MI); Masters in leadership & Nonprofit Management (Regis University - Denver, CO); Doctorate in Ministry (Destiny Christian University – Winter-haven, FL). Also, a Diploma in Biblical Studies (RHEMA Correspondence Bible School -Tulsa, OK). She lives in Michigan and she enjoys reading, writing, walking, and serving others through servant leadership.

NOTES...

If you would like to receive The Ultimate Person who can give you Joy, please say this prayer out loud:

Father God it is written in Your Word that if I confess with my mouth that Jesus is Lord and believe in my heart that You raised Him from the dead I shall be saved from eternal hell. Therefore, I confess Jesus is Lord and I make Him Lord of my life right now. I renounce my past life and I close the door to any sins and desires that are not like Christ. I thank You for forgiving me of all my sins and Jesus is now my Lord and my Savior. I am a now a new creation. Old things have passed away and all things have become new in Jesus' name. Amen!

Congratulations you are now born again!
Continue in this Happy New Life!

For other Books and Materials

by

Dr. Christine Renee

visit HARPublishing.com

or

www.DrChristineRenee.com